RUSSIAN GLASS

OF THE 17TH–20TH CENTURIES

"Russian Glass of the 17th–20th Centuries"
A special exhibition
The Corning Museum of Glass
Corning, New York
April 22–October 14, 1990

This exhibition is funded, in part, by grants from the
National Endowment for the Arts and the New York
State Council on the Arts.

Cover: Vase. Imperial Glassworks, 1830–1840.

Design: Mary Lou Littrell
Typography: Brookside Typographers, Inc.
Printing: Village Craftsmen, Inc./Princeton Polychrome Press

Standard Book Number 0-87290-123-8
Library of Congress Catalog Card Number 89-081837

Editor's note: The transliteration of Russian
names has followed, wherever possible, those
given in the *Encyclopaedia Britannica* (1973 edition)
and the *National Geographic Atlas of the World*
(1970 edition).

RUSSIAN GLASS
OF THE 17TH–20TH CENTURIES

Dr. Nina Asharina
Vice Director, The State History Museum, Moscow

Dr. Tamara Malinina
Curator of Russian Glass, The State Hermitage Museum, Leningrad

Dr. Liudmila Kazakova
Historian of Art, Academy of Arts, Moscow

The Corning Museum of Glass
Corning, New York

Contents

The Glass Bead Room in Catherine the Great's Chinese Pavilion at Oranienbaum (now Lomonosov), near Leningrad, about 1762–1764. The background of the embroidered hangings, designed by Giuseppe and Serafino Barozzi, is covered with glass beads. Photo by Tim Imrie, courtesy Country Life Library.

Foreword

EVER SINCE THE CORNING MUSEUM OF GLASS opened in 1951, its staff has been interested in glass made in Russia. Our first acquisitions included examples of 19th-century Russian glass. During the last 39 years, the collections have been enriched with further acquisitions, many of them gifts, which allow us to demonstrate modestly the history of glassmaking in Russia from the beginning of the 18th century to the present.

When compared to the collections in the Soviet Union, however, our holdings pale. We decided nearly 10 years ago that a special exhibition of glass made in Russia should be presented in Corning, and that we would try to interest colleagues in Russian museums in sharing their treasures temporarily with Americans.

The response to our invitation was beyond our wildest hopes. Our Russian colleagues greeted the idea enthusiastically, opened their displays and storerooms to us, and eagerly shared their knowledge of Russian glassmaking history. By endeavoring to find the best objects to illustrate particularly important points, and by selecting the most important and beautiful examples available, they have permitted us to present the first comprehensive exhibition of Russian glass ever shown in the West.

Several objects that we would have loved to include in the exhibition could not be sent to Corning for a variety of reasons. Some of these works illustrated in this catalog were too big or too fragile to be shipped safely. Others, such as the Bead Room at Catherine the Great's Chinese Pavilion at Oranienbaum near Leningrad (illustrated on page 6), obviously could not be included. There is, however, much in the show and in this catalog that will delight and often amaze.

Organizing this exhibition was not a one-person job, and many colleagues contributed significantly to its success. One person who deserves our greatest gratitude is Dr. Nina Asharina. She supervised the preparation of the catalog and the exhibition, wrote much of the text, arranged for the photography of objects located in museums and galleries hundreds of miles apart, and convinced hesitant curators to lend their most important glass. The success of this catalog and the exhibition it documents is largely a testament to her skill, good humor, and dedication. The other authors of the catalog text, Tamara Malinina and Liudmila Kazakova, also demonstrated their profound understanding of their subject, and their unflagging enthusiasm for the project kept it moving ahead.

The Russian glass exhibition and an exchange exhibition on American glassmaking history (the latter will be shown in Moscow, Leningrad, and Tallinn) were organized under the auspices of the Ministry of Culture in Moscow. With the strong commitment of Dr. Henrikh P. Popov, chief of the Department of Fine Arts and Monuments Protection, and Vladimir Litvinov of the Department of Foreign Relations, the agreements were made and signed. The energetic Lidija Zaljetova of the Department of Fine Arts at the Ministry of Culture ably organized several visits to artists and displays of contemporary glass in far-flung parts of the Soviet Union. She also served as the principal liaison in the Ministry, allowing us to see thousands of works by today's leading artists before making our selection for the exhibition. We owe each of the glassmakers and glass collectors we visited—who lavished us with spectacular feasts!—a note of thanks. We are also grateful to Irina Mikheyeva for her willing assistance on several occasions. And to the translators who helped us mightily on our planning visits, especially Oleg Smirnoff and Igor Kozlov.

The directors and curators of the lending museums deserve our special thanks, for without their assistance, this exhibition could not take place. For their help, and for permitting us to examine objects on display and to visit storage areas, we are truly indebted. Those who deserve particular recognition are:

At the State Hermitage Museum, Leningrad: Academic Boris Piotrovsky, director, Dr. Vitali A. Souslov, vice director, Dr. Irina N. Ouchanova, Dr. Tamara Malinina, and Dr. Olga Michailova.

At the State Russian Museum: Dr. Vladimir A. Gusev, director, Dr. Irina Popova, vice director, Elena Ivanova, and Dr. Evgenia Petrova.

At the State History Museum: Prof. Konstantin Levikin, director, Dr. Nina Asharina, vice director, Dr. Nina P. Sorokina, Inna I. Sergeenko, Alexey Zaitsev, and Tamara Igumnova.

At the Vladimir-Suzdal Artistic Museum, Dr. Alisa I. Aksenova, director, and at the glass museum department at Gus' Khrustal'nyy, Victorije Ugrumova, chief.

At the Pavlovsk Palace Museum, Mrs. Nesterova Eleonora, chief curator.

At the Museum of the State Glass Institute, Moscow: Svetlana Zhuravleva, Irina Polianskaia, and Natalia Smoliakova.

At the State Armory Museum, Moscow: Liudmilla Frolova and Irina Polinina.

At the Museum of Applied Arts, Tallinn, Estonia: Marika Valk, director, and Anne Tiivel.

Particular thanks are due the Hon. Jack Matlock, the United States Ambassador to the Soviet Union, and his wife, Rebecca, who took a personal interest in these exchange exhibitions and helped to guarantee that they would take place. Both of them were helpful and thoughtful advisers when sound counsel was needed. Nowhere has there been a more appreciated "home away from home" than Spaso House, which they kindly opened to us.

Finally, there are several other Americans who have played key roles in this project: Richard and Mary O'Brien arranged our first, crucial contacts with the Ministry of Culture, and they repeatedly arranged key meetings for us during the years that we have been working on the exhibitions. Congressman Amory Houghton, Jr. (then chairman of Corning Glass Works), who with Richard O'Brien independently thought of presenting a Russian glass exhibition in Corning, set the wheels in motion. Ann Miller and Margot Mininni-Aldriedge, who helped us with on-the-spot contacts with our Soviet colleagues. Colleagues William F. Hutton, senior curator of The Toledo Museum of Art (with which we are allied in the exchange exhibition), and Susanne K. Frantz, curator of 20th-century glass at The Corning Museum of Glass, traveled to the Soviet Union to help select the glass. Roger Mandle, then director of The Toledo Museum of Art, spurred us into action on the exhibitions and joined with Corning in committing our Museums' treasures of American glass to a traveling exhibition in the USSR.

The year 1990 promises to be one of momentous change in relations between the United States and the Soviet Union. We are proud to be part of the exchange of objects and ideas that is helping us better understand American and Russian history and achievements, and we are thrilled to have the honor of showing the great treasures of Russian glass.

Dwight P. Lanmon
Director
The Corning Museum of Glass

Glassmaking in Russia in the 17th and 18th Centuries

Nina Asharina

THE HISTORY OF GLASSMAKING in Russia is divided into two periods. The first goes back to the early Middle Ages, and the second embraces modern times.

The first glassmaking furnaces and homemade articles of glass were discovered during archeological excavations in cities in the territory of the Kiev Rus. Between the ninth and the 13th centuries, this territory stretched from the Carpathians in the west to the upper reaches of the river Volga in the east. The production of blown glass vessels, window glass, and various women's ornaments of colored glass—beads, bracelets, and rings—was mastered and well established in Rus in the 11th–13th centuries. The palette of colored glass was extensive. It included violet, yellow, blue, turquoise, black, green, brown, and red.

In the 13th century, tragic events interrupted the natural development of Russian glassmaking. Kiev Rus, exhausted by the internecine strife of its princes, was defeated and enslaved by the Tatar-Mongols. Many cities where trade and crafts had flourished were destroyed. Thousands of artisans were executed or taken prisoner. The nearly three centuries of the rule of the Golden Horde inflicted grave damage on the political, economic, and cultural development of ancient Rus. Meanwhile, the western Russian lands were ruled by the Great Lithuanian Principality and later by Poland. Placed in different historical circumstances, the formerly integral Russian ethnic group, which had a common language and culture, split into three branches: Russian, Belorussian, and Ukrainian.

Moscow Rus, having freed itself from foreign domination earlier than other territories and restored its statehood, pursued a consistent policy aimed at reunification with the Ukraine and Belorussia. This process, which started in the 1500s, was completed only by the end of the 18th century. Thus, Russian, Ukrainian, and Belorussian glassmaking had a common origin, but developed with a degree of independence stemming from the different historical destinies of the three nations.

In the 17th century, the emerging Russian nation was gaining strength. It was a time when the new and the old, the progressive and the conservative, were closely connected. The intensive development of crafts led to the emergence of the first manufactories. The growth of production provided an impetus to trade, which linked the formerly isolated economic areas into an integrated national market. Later, Russia reunited with the Ukraine and Belorussia. This was an event of major political importance—an event that helped to expand the ties between Moscow Rus and European countries.

The fresh demand for window glass, which replaced mica in wealthy Russian homes, was met chiefly by imports from Livonia and Little Russia (the Ukraine), where production was based on the traditions and experience of the glassmakers of Kiev Rus. These areas sent 80,000 to 90,000 windowpanes to Moscow every year. Luxury items of Venetian glass came either as ambassadorial gifts or through the port of Archangel, which linked Moscow Rus with western European countries. Such luxuries, however, formed only a small part of its trade.

On March 2, 1630, the cannon maker Yuli Koyet arrived in Moscow. Two years later, he invited Paul Kunckel, an experienced glassmaker who had set up a glassworks in Sweden, to help him select a site for a glasshouse. In 1634, Koyet received a license to erect a glass factory in the village of Dukhanino in the Dmitrov district, not far from Moscow. The construction took five years, and Russia's first glassworks began commercial operation in 1639. The workshop was very small. Only six to eight craftsmen could work in it at one time, and production was limited to the summer months. All of the workers were foreigners, and they returned home when their contracts expired.

Since there was a chronic shortage of craftsmen, the glasshouse often remained idle, and Yuli Koyet's heirs, who operated the factory, experienced serious financial difficulties. As a result, they had to sell half of the glassworks. Their first partner was Ivan Falki, a gunpowder and bell maker, who was succeeded by his daughter and in the 1690s by a foreign merchant named Andrei Minter. Minter was last mentioned in 1754, and in 1760, the craftsmen of the Dukhanino Works were attached to Akim Maltsov's workshop in Gus "by a decree of the College of Manufactories."

Thus, the first enterprise of the Russian glassmaking industry existed for nearly 120 years. Naturally, it underwent considerable changes during that time. While it originally had six to eight craftsmen working just 25 to 30 weeks a year, the number of workers eventually reached 32. Throughout its history, the factory's principal products were window glass and pharmaceutical vessels. After 1725, it also produced "bucket, half bucket, and quart bottles." In the 1730s, the glasshouse began to make colorless glass, which was engraved, cut, and faceted in Moscow.

Another private glassworks was built by Von-Sweden in the Kashira district in 1666 for the making of glass in "the Venetian style." When the owner died two years later, production ceased.

The glasshouse founded in the village of Izmailovo near Moscow (now part of the city) at the initiative of Czar Alexis I in 1668 played a major role in the history of Russian glassmaking. Its furnaces produced the first truly Russian glass, and the manufactory also served as a school of glassmaking. Russian, Ukrainian, and foreign craftsmen were trained there. Many of the latter continued to live and work in Russia.

The glassworks was intended for the making of tableware for the czar's court, and its founders brought in the best foreign craftsmen. The construction of the factory involved a foreigner, Ivan Martynov, and two Russians, Boris Ivanov and Grigory Vasilyev. Later,

1. Czar Alexis I
(Alexey Mikhailovich).
Portrait: unknown artist,
end of the 17th century,
courtesy of State History
Museum, Moscow.

Christian Kunckel, Ivan Yakovlev, and Mark Ivanov worked there. It is hard for us to judge the nature of their labor, but they were probably builders because other craftsmen arrived in 1670 to replace them. They were called "Venetians," evidently not because of their nationality but because of the style of their work. Ian Artsypukhor, Indrik Lerin, Peter Baltus, and Lovis Moet probably came to the Izmailovo glasshouse from the Netherlands, where glassmaking "in the Venetian style" flourished in the 17th century. Baltus is mentioned in documents dating back to 1688, when he was sent to the Netherlands to purchase various materials. Lerin, who must have come to Russia as a young man, spent more than 40 years at the glassworks, leaving it only after the production of luxury glassware had stopped. This means that he took part in all of the refined glassmaking activity there. The fact that masters stayed at the glasshouse for a long time helps to explain the durability of its traditions, which determined the style of Russian glassmaking for many years thereafter. Foreign masters brought their own recipes for melting glass and techniques for working it, which they adapted to local materials and taste.

The Izmailovo glassworks specialized in the manufacture of luxury items for the court, and produced very little for the domestic market. The list of its products is long and contains the names of objects traditionally made in pottery and metal. Nevertheless, the inventories also mention such unusual objects as a "long, amusing goblet" and a "church chandelier with figurines." These works are more decorative than utilitarian in nature. Their new shapes and large size were designed to elicit the surprise and admiration of the czar and his courtiers, who were very fond of curiosities of every kind. In addition, the factory records frequently mention "striped," "small," and large-scale tumblers, pitchers, and bottles of "white" (i.e., colorless) glass.

Among the collections of the State Historical Museum in Moscow is a group of objects that, with a certain degree of caution, can be attributed to the Izmailovo glassworks. These products include a ewer (*kumgan*). The glass surface is molded in an allover diamond pattern, and the spout ends in the head of a ram (no. 1). It is likely that the ewer and the "amusing" beakers were made by the "master of figurines," Indrik Lerin, who was employed at the glasshouse from 1670 to 1711. He received the nickname "Venetian" because the style of his work closely resembled glass "in the Venetian style," which was then being made in many European countries.

During the 17th century, the Venetian style of glassmaking began to be replaced by the Bohemian style of engraved glass. The managers of the Izmailovo glassworks shared this passion for the new mode of ornamentation. However, Hans Friedrich, a "master of the cutting business" who was working in the factory in 1673, failed to change the nature of its products substantially. For example, the receipt book of the glassworks for 1677 listed only "two cut and 15 faceted wineglasses" out of a total of 9,246 items. Another master, Matthias Ulmann, was more productive. He came to the glasshouse in late 1680 and stayed there for more than 20 years. Other products of the Izmailovo factory were gilded and the "gold painter" Dmitry Stepanov decorated various drug vessels for the czar's court.

Izmailovo glass was highly valued. It was used daily by the czar's family and courtiers, and it was sold at the Gostiny Dvor, a well-known row of shops in Moscow. The phrase "made in Izmailovo" was sufficient even for the clerks, who usually went out of their way to give detailed descriptions. It signified not only the high quality of the glass but also the style of the ornament. This "Izmailovo style" of design continued even after the glasshouse itself had been closed down. For example, the inventories of the Zhabino glassworks in 1730 listed beer tumblers made from "imperial material" in the "Izmailovo style." Indeed, the traditions of the Izmailovo factory exerted a decisive influence on Russian glassmaking. They were followed for an especially long time by the 18th-century Russian folk craftsmen who made figured glasses.

Information about another 17th-century Russian glassworks—in the village of Voskre-senskoye in the Chernogolovskoye rural district—is extremely scanty. Nothing is known about the length of its existence or what was made there. Information on this factory goes back only to 1687, when it was already in operation and its products were being sold at the Gostiny Dvor in Moscow. Among these items were tumblers, *bratina*s, and icon lamps. It appears that this factory was a branch of the Izmailovo glassworks because its products are included in the Izmailovo inventory.

Thus, in the late 17th century, there were three glassworks near Moscow: Dukhanino, Zhabino, and Voskresenskoye. All of them were rather small, and clearly they could not supply the entire country with glass.

The construction of a fourth state-owned glassworks began in 1691. Its supervision was entrusted to the "merchant of the Gostiny Dvor hundred," Yakov Romanov, who built the factory at the Tainitskiye Gates in Moscow. However, the project collapsed because Romanov failed to find skilled craftsmen able to start up production.

After this failure, the Moscow administration started to build a new mirror factory in Vorob'yevo, having invited the commissioner Brockhausen from Berlin to oversee the work. He came to Moscow in 1705 with six French mirror makers he had hired. He may also have brought some of the equipment. The factory opened in 1706. There were interruptions in production, evidently because the foreign craftsmen could not adapt to using the local raw materials at once. The clerk Postnikov, who oversaw their work, reported that they failed to justify their salaries because they withheld the secrets of their craft from the Russian glassmakers and because only one out of 10 glass pots produced good glass. In 1706, seven apprentices from Izmailovo were sent to the Vorob'yevo factory to improve its operation, even though Izmailovo itself was short of skilled workmen. The Vorob'yevo works employed 18 people in all.

The craftsmen at Vorob'yevo made mirrors not only by the traditional method of blowing, but also by casting them on a copper bed specially made for the purpose. These mirrors were rather large by 18th century standards. Some of them reached 2.8 meters in length and 1.4 meters in width. Many were mounted in glass frames. In 1712, the factory was making mirrors, several kinds of dishes, decanters of different sizes, and bells.

To complete this review of Russian glassmaking in the late 17th and early 18th centuries, we must mention yet another area where the industry was concentrated. Nine small glasshouses operated in the Trubchevsk, Sevsk, and Karachayevsk districts (now the Bryansk region) from 1706 to 1718. They made "simple blown glass" and "white and simple glass."

In the second decade of the 18th century, St. Petersburg became the new center of Russian glassmaking. Two glassworks were established near the city. One was located in the town of Yamburg, and the other was in the village of Zhabino. One can only guess when they were founded because no early records have survived. The workshops were mentioned for the first time in 1717 when the owner, Prince A. D. Menshikov, made plans to lease them. The information is unclear and contradictory, but we believe that both factories were built by Swedes, from whom the ancient Russian town of Yam (Yamburg) had been recaptured in 1703 during the Northern War. It was no accident that the glasshouses were part of Prince Menshikov's property. The town of Yamburg was among the huge estates granted to him in Ingermanland. A register, in which the output of dishes at the Zhabino glassworks in 1717 was recorded, is preserved at the Historical Museum. We learn from it that the products included pitchers, wineglasses, flasks, tumblers, and colorless lamps for icons. The register also records the production of dishes of blue glass.

Documents of 1728–1730 contain more detailed information about the Yamburg and Zhabino glasshouses, which became state property when Menshikov fell into disgrace. At the time, the two factories already had 91 employees, many of whom had worked at the Vorob'yevo mirror factory. The Yamburg glassworks was larger than its counterpart in Zhabino, and its production was better organized. It made mirror and window glass as well as cut and engraved "crystal dishes" that accounted for nearly a third of its total output. From 1713, the engraving of dishes was done by the foreign master Johann Mennart, who abandoned his craft in 1723 because of an eye disease. He was replaced by two Russian engravers, the apprentices Dementy Voilokov and Vasily Pivovarov, who later became masters.

The Yamburg glasshouse catered chiefly to the palaces, supplying window glass, mirrors, and "crystal" vessels for the new imperial residences. Some of its products were sold both at the factory and at the palace shop. In 1730, however, the demand for mirrors and glass declined because Emperor Peter II (1727–1730) moved his residence from St. Petersburg to Moscow.

After 1730, the Yamburg and Zhabino glassworks were leased to William Elmzel. They closed about 1733–1735.

Engraved goblets and wineglasses figure prominently among the products of the Yamburg glasshouse. Their decoration was largely limited to nationalistic emblems and inscriptions. The inscription "Vivat (long live) Czar Peter Alekseevich" was particularly widespread during the reign of Peter the Great, who died in 1725 (no. 2). Portraying the reigning monarch on glass was widely practiced at the Yamburg factory. Such goblets and wineglasses were probably given as presents. Goblets with profiles of Empress Anna Ivanovna (1730–1740, no. 3) are found in museums more often than vessels with other portraits. The shape of these goblets is simple enough: a stately, baluster-shaped, and slightly faceted stem and a bowl with faceted arched ovals on its base. This design proved very durable, and it is characteristic of products from the Yamburg glassworks. The engraving also has a number of distinctive features. The portrait of the empress is very schematic. While reproducing the details of the dress and the hairstyle with loving care, the engraver failed to convey an accurate likeness. Branches of butterfly leaves and daisies frame medallions with the portrait and a heraldic eagle. It is believed that this particular goblet was engraved by one of the Russian masters at the factory, either Vasily Pivovarov or Dementy Voilokov.

The history of the St. Petersburg Glassworks, the most important of the 18th-century Russian glasshouses, began in a somewhat unusual manner. Its existence on the banks of the Fontanka River, almost in the heart of the city, is first documented in 1738, when its founder, William Elmzel, died. The masters and the tools had been brought there from the Yamburg factory. However, judging by the inventories, this in fact was a cutting shop, where objects were cut, polished, and engraved, and not a glassworks.

After the workshop had been turned over to the state, it became a glasshouse where vessels were blown and plate glass was cast, polished, and engraved. Some of its products were made to order for the imperial court, and others were put on sale. Glassware was sold in a shop on Nevsky Avenue and at the factory itself. The cutting shop was run by Joseph Piltz and Vasily Pivovarov, who had seven apprentices under their supervision. A new specialist craft—cutting vessels—appeared at the glassworks at that time. Previously, vessels had been ground by the same masters who cut and polished the mirrors; now, there were nine vessel cutters, directed by Kuzma Zerchaninov.

In 1774, the glassworks was moved to the village of Naziya in the Schlüsselburg district, while a workshop was to be left in St. Petersburg for "cutting vessels and engraving emblems and monograms on them." However, it is evident from the memoirs of the diplomat Franz Carberon that, as late as 1780, this decision had not been carried out, and that the cutting shop continued to operate at the glasshouse.

Many products of the St. Petersburg factory survive. These are chiefly goblets, beakers, tumblers, vodka bottles (*shtofs*), and teapots. They attest vividly to the vitality of engraving at that time. In fact, the cutters at the glassworks did much more than engrave emblems and monograms. They developed intricate rococo ornaments, architectural landscapes, portraits, allegorical compositions, and gallant and pastoral scenes. Every engraver had his favorite subjects and characteristic styles. Inevitably, the presence of foreign engravers was reflected in the character of the decoration, which in many ways resembles the Bohemian, Silesian, and Saxon styles. However, the presence of these different influences imparted a unique character to the glass of St. Petersburg. In addition, the Russian masters interpreted the foreign styles in their own way while remaining faithful to traditional tastes both in the choice of subjects and in the composition of their engravings. Much was also determined by the orders from the imperial court, which reflected the tastes and moods there.

The glassblowers were less constrained than the cutters, since they had the benefit of a century's accumulated experience. This explains why the shapes of the goblets, tumblers, and vodka bottles from the St. Petersburg Glassworks are very distinctive in their sizes, proportions, and forms (nos. 4–8).

Another distinctive feature of the glass made at St. Petersburg was the combination of engraving with gilding and niello. This resulted in particularly beautiful goblets. Their style is baroque. Goblets usually bore engraved half-length portraits of Empress Elizabeth Petrovna and, from 1762, Empress Catherine II. These portraits, carefully reproduced from medals and coins, are overwhelmed by luxuriant cartouches consisting of heavy canopies supported by putti, as can be seen in a goblet (no. 6) in the collection of the Historical Museum. The portrait of Empress Elizabeth Petrovna wearing a black wig is not a product of the artist's imagination; it reflects actual observation at the imperial court.

During the reign of Catherine II (1762–1796), imperial portraits on glass often appeared in allegorical compositions celebrating the deeds of the enlightened empress. A goblet in the collection of the Historical Museum, decorated with deep cutting, is a striking case in point (no. 8). Deep engraved waves sweep over the entire surface. In the storm, two tritons carry a shell in which Neptune lies in a contorted pose, supporting a portrait of Catherine II. Two ships are also shown. One of them, flying a Turkish flag, is in distress. This allegory may refer to Russia's victories at sea in the Russo-Turkish War (1768–1774). While the style of engraving is baroque or rococo art in character, the nature of the allegory and the system of images used make it more akin to the emerging neo-classical style.

More than 80 private glassworks were built in Russia during the 1700s. In the first half of the 18th century, these factories were centered in the environs of Moscow. Besides the Dukhanino glasshouse, which was already in operation, five glasshouses were built there before 1725. One of these, the factory in the Mozhaysk district, deserves special mention. It was here that the "glassmaking empire" of the Maltsovs originated. The Maltsov family monopolized glass production in Russia between the 18th and the early 20th centuries. The glassworks was founded in 1723 by Nazar Druzhinin and Sergei Aksenov, who made the merchant Vasili Maltsov their partner in the following year. At that time, the three owners employed just seven workers. Maltsov, who became the sole owner in 1730, energetically began to expand production. By 1738, the Mozhaysk factory had turned into one of the major enterprises of the Russian glass industry. It had four furnaces in which simple green glass was melted and two furnaces for colorless glass. Five workshops with 50 wheels for grinding and polishing mirrors were built. There were also three additional rooms with 14 wheels for polishing, and eight more wheels were set aside for grinding. However, this well-equipped glassworks was short of skilled workmen, and as a result, many tools stood idle. To amend this situation, Timofey Scherbakov and Afanasy Nekrasov, two veterans of Russian glassmaking, were invited to join the factory. They had previously worked both at the Vorob'yevo mirror factory near Moscow and at the Yamburg glasshouse.

In 1730, Vasili Maltsov signed a contract with three Bohemian masters: the glassblower Matthius Tomasevich, the grinder Joseph Stark, and the engraver Joseph Genkin. Genkin stayed at the Maltsov factory from 1730 until 1737, when he moved to Gottlieb Stenzel's factory in Dukhanino.

Samples of Maltsov glass submitted to the College of Manufactories in 1745 were highly praised, and Maltsov was permitted to put his trademark on them. However, this was rarely done and only three signed pieces are known. As a result, it is now very difficult to determine which engraved glasses can be attributed to the Maltsovs. According to the records, the Maltsov glassworks in Mozhaysk made vodka bottles, tumblers, wine-glasses, and beakers of colorless glass, which were engraved and sometimes gilded. The main motifs were monograms of Empress Elizabeth Petrovna and Russian two-headed eagles, for which the workmen received five kopecks. Goblets with "emblems" were also popular. A typical specimen of Maltsov's production is a goblet with gilded engraving that shows a running wounded deer and the inscription "A Flight from Illness" (no. 9). The subject was borrowed from the published collection *Symbols and Emblems*. This collection, extremely popular in Russia, was printed in Amsterdam in 1705 at the order of Peter the Great. Later, it was republished in Russia many times, and its illustrations served as design sources for Russian pewter, silver, and glass decorators.

The goblet may have been engraved by Stepan Lagutin, who began to work at the Maltsov glasshouse in 1732. He was trained by Joseph Genkin and later replaced him as the leading master. The dramatic events in his life help us to trace the histories of the Russian factories where glass was engraved. In 1740, Lagutin followed Genkin in moving to Gottlieb Stenzel's (formerly Koyet's) glasshouse in Dukhanino. Later, he worked in Moscow, at Pyotr Nechayev's factory in Yaroslavl' (1743), and at Matvei Lonkarev's glassworks in the Mozhaysk district (1748). From 1749 to 1761, Lagutin was again at the Maltsov factory, and from 1766 to 1775, he worked at the Bakhmetiev glasshouse near Penza. This chronology shows that in the first half of the 18th century, glass was engraved in Russia in at least four private factories besides those in Yamburg and St. Petersburg. Later, they were joined by two more glassworks owned by the Nemchinovs in the Dorogobuzh district (founded in 1748) and in the Gzhatsk district (founded in 1761) of the province of Smolensk, as well as by the Bakhmetiev factory at Nikol'skoye in Penza province in 1764.

Maltsov's production also expanded considerably. In 1746, he started to construct a second glasshouse in the village of Novoye. Two years later, there were 160 workmen at the two Maltsov factories. Among them were Maltsov's own serfs. However, an imperial decree of 1747, which prohibited the building of glass and iron works near Moscow and St. Petersburg, damaged this flourishing enterprise. To preserve forests near the two capitals, orders were issued to move the existing glassworks at least 200 kilometers away from them.

In 1746, Vasili Maltsov turned over the management of his two glasshouses to his sons Akim and Alexander. Reluctantly obeying the decree, they divided the factories and began to look for new locations for them. In 1750, Alexander Maltsov moved his part of the glassworks to the Trubchevsk district of Oryol province in the southwest, where his descendants built several more glasshouses before the end of the century. These included the Dyat'kovo Crystal Works, which is still the largest in Russia.

Akim Maltsov left the old glassworks in 1755. Unlike his brother, he moved to the northeast, where he established his factory on the Gus River in Vladimir province in 1756. This factory, which led to the creation of the town of Gus' Khrustal'nyy, is the oldest Russian glasshouse in operation today.

By the end of the 18th century, the three branches of the Maltsov family owned a total of 16 glassworks in the Vladimir, Kaluga, and Oryol provinces. These provinces became the focus of glassmaking in Russia in the late 18th and 19th centuries. Similarly intensive construction of glass factories also occurred in other areas. Some of these businesses operated until the end of the 19th century, while others closed down after 20 or 30 years. In all, there were 54 Russian glasshouses functioning in 1800, although more than 80 had been built in the last hundred years. Only a small number of these factories made luxury tableware: five of the Maltsov works, the two owned by the Nemchinovs, and the Yamburg, St. Petersburg (later Imperial), Bakhmetiev, and Orlov glasshouses.

The vast majority of Russia's private glassworks produced simple objects for everyday use or vessels of unpurified green glass. They made a standard range of products: jugs for water and beer, vodka flasks, and bottles of various shapes and sizes. Other vessels, wash jugs, small casks, flasks, and bottles shaped like animals and birds were made less frequently. Much of this "folk glass" was enameled. Eventually, it acquired the status of works of art and was placed in private and museum collections.

The State Historical Museum has the largest collection of "folk glass." It consists of 300 items and represents all the shapes of vessels used in everyday life in 18th-century Russia. The green glass jugs are notable for their impressive size, and the earliest ones repeat the outlines of ceramic objects. Later, a form more adapted to the glassblowing technique was developed.

The collection contains many bottles, which were a staple of every Russian glassworks in the 1700s. Only two types are known. The first type, a flask with a tall, narrow neck, was common only in the first half of the century. The second type, which was almost cylindrical and also had a tall, narrow neck, survived until the mid-1800s. Bottles differed chiefly in their sizes, which were related to the capacity of the measuring bucket (about 10 liters). There were bottles containing a full, half, quarter, and eighth bucket.

The production of *shtof*s (four-sided vodka bottles with a capacity of three pounds) was particularly large in the 18th century. Half *shtof*s are also known.

Bottles in the form of animals and birds are more than purely utilitarian forms. They represent a kind of glass sculpture that retains functional elements. The figure of a dancing bear is one example. Made in a simple and generalized manner, it resembles the hero of Russian street entertainments staged by wandering actors (no. 10). When portraying animals in glass, Russian masters carefully chose the most characteristic details, which enabled them to create convincing images with just a few elements.

Most of the surviving 18th-century green glass bottles and jugs are painted with opaque colored enamels. Decorators used five colors: white, red, blue, green, and yellow. Significantly, a similar range of colors was employed in 17th-century Russian tiles used to decorate the facades of buildings.

The decoration of a glass object usually consisted to two elements: a plant and an animal. Inscriptions with the names of the owners or dates are also common.

Most of the decoration found on green glass was painted with swift, confident brush-strokes. The usual ornament shows two branches with an abundance of lush leaves. One branch bends under the weight of a red tulip, the other under a carnation. These branches form a kind of cartouche that contains the main picture. This type of ornamentation goes back to the 17th-century "grass patterns" often found on Russian tiles, carved wooden screens for displaying icons, book drawings, and textiles.

The world of animals and birds represented in glass paintings is limited. Decorators often depicted lions, griffins, cranes, and storks, and occasionally painted horses and bears. These figures usually have freely painted red outlines, with yellow indicating the manes or feathers. All of the animals are in profile. The lions and griffins frozen in threatening poses (no. 11) are particularly impressive, with tails that turn into stalks with flowers. These mythological images are widely known in other types of Russian applied art (e.g., relief tiles and paintings on wood).

Holiday scenes (no. 12) were another popular topic for paintings on green glass. The usual figures in them are a lady with a beaker in her hand, an admirer, and a violinist. Evidently, this subject, unknown in earlier Russian art, was borrowed from the decorative arts of Europe. In the first half of the 18th century, these scenes were delineated on a large scale. The figures ride in carriages or dance, and their clothes correspond closely to the fashions of the period. By the middle of the century, however, the scenes had lost their dynamic character, the number of figures was reduced, and their attire had become more democratic. In these figures, one can easily recognize middle-class Russian towns-people. Undoubtedly, this is a transformation of the "gallant scenes" into the picture of a traditional Russian ritual in which the hostess brought a glass of wine to her guests of honor and then allowed them to kiss her.

Green glass with enamel decoration belongs to the folk craft of Russian towns. In the 18th century, Russian urban culture lost its homogeneity. The reforms of Peter the Great, who made Europeanization a part of national policy, produced a clear dividing line between elite and folk culture. Professional art developed within the framework of such European styles as baroque, rococo, and neo-classicism. Folk art, on the other hand, developed within a Russian tradition, seemingly without any apparent stylistic rules. In fact, however, folk artists adapted the baroque style. A similar situation occurred in the realm of engraved glass at private glassworks in the second half of the 18th century. Their engravings, which came more and more to resemble folk art, were still based on the baroque style at the end of the 18th century.

The neo-classical style in 18th-century Russian glass developed gradually, with the introduction of elements that slightly altered the baroque designs. Russian glass that was truly neo-classical appeared only in the last three decades of the 18th century. This style was used in a particularly expressive and original manner in the colored glass of the St. Petersburg and Bakhmetiev glassworks.

In the first half of the 18th century, when colorless engraved glass was at the height of its popularity, masters at Russian glasshouses experimented with colored glass. For instance, we learn from the register at the Zhabino factory near St. Petersburg that in 1717 the glasshouse made "blue" glass, from which cups, saucers, and trays were blown.

Other information about colored glass dates back to 1741, when Ivan Konerev, master at the St. Petersburg Glassworks and one in a long line of glassmakers, reported that he could make colorless, green, red, black, white, cornflower blue, and cherry-colored glass. However, it was a long time before his discoveries entered production. Thus, in 1751, the St. Petersburg factory's principal products were still colorless glass, green bottle glass, and blue glass.

In the 1740s, the eminent Russian scientist Mikhail Lomonosov began to conduct intensive research on the production of colored glass. He also celebrated this remarkable material in poetic form, devoting "A Message on the Usefulness of Glass" to it. Pyotr Druzhinin, who was sent for training to Lomonosov in 1752, returned to the St. Petersburg glasshouse the following year to organize the production of colored glass. He remained there until 1773. The manager of that glasshouse, Lilienthal, reported in 1770 that Druzhinin and two other masters, Sidor Yurasov and Ivan Khrypov, could make colored glass.

Besides turning over his recipes for colored glass to the St. Petersburg Glassworks, in 1752 Lomonosov founded his own factory at Ust' Ruditsa near the capital for making of mosaic tesserae, beads, and tubular ('bugle') beads. The tesserae were produced mainly for the mosaic workshop of the Academy of Sciences, which made about 40 mosaics during its 20 years of existence. Among them, Lomonosov's own works are of particular interest and significance. They include *The Savior Not Made by Human Hand* (1753), a portrait of Peter the Great (1755–1757), and the enormous *Battle of Poltava* (1761–1764). A mosaic portrait of P. I. Shuvalov (no. 13) was made at Lomonosov's workshop by Matvey Vasilyev, Yefim Melnikov, and Ignat Petrov in 1758.

Tesserae from the Ust' Ruditsa factory were used in finishing the Chinese Palace in Oranienbaum near St. Petersburg, which was designed by the architect A. Rinaldi in 1762–1764. They were also employed to create the floor in the "bugle study" and to decorate consoles at the Peterhof lapidary works.

Bugles and beads made at Lomonosov's factory were widely used for decorating such household items as panels, clothing, furniture, purses, and beadwork sleeves for tumblers, decanters, and candlesticks. While the patterns were sometimes simple, objects with designs worked by hand were favored for special gifts. In the second half of the

2. Vase.
Blown, gilded bronze mounts.
St. Petersburg Glassworks, second half of the 18th century.
H. 105 cm. State Hermitage Museum, Leningrad.

18th century, beads and bugles were used to ornament the frames of icons—a continuation of the long tradition of studding the robes of icons with pearls and precious stones (no. 14).

Lomonosov's factory also made various dishes of turquoise, blue, and white glass, as well as "colored (marble) dishes" and all kinds of costume jewelry. The lapidary Grigoryev was trained to insert colored tesserae into finger rings.

After Lomonosov's death, the Ust' Ruditsa factory survived only until 1768. Tesserae for mosaics were then being made by the master Prokhor Kurilov of the St. Petersburg Glassworks. The destinies of the two enterprises had been closely linked. Lomonosov and the St. Petersburg masters had worked side by side to develop recipes for making colored glass and plans for expanding its production.

The St. Petersburg Glassworks became the leader in the manufacture of Russian colored glass for household needs. However, as mentioned above, in 1774 the factory was moved to the town of Naziya in the Schlüsselburg district, although for some time the cutting and engraving workshop remained in St. Petersburg. In 1777, Catherine II transferred the glasshouse to her favorite, G. A. Potemkin, for "perpetual and hereditary ownership." Potemkin moved the factory from Naziya to the village of Ozerki near St. Petersburg in 1783. Following his death in 1792, the glasshouse again became state property and was renamed the Imperial Glassworks. It was managed until 1802 by Prince N. B. Yusupov, who reorganized it into one of the best glassworks not only in Russia but also in Europe.

In addition to colorless glass, the factory produced colored items of "white, violet, ivory, scarlet, yellow, blue, green, and marbled glass." Colored glass was widely used both for tableware and for interior decoration. The chief master of the works, Yefrem Karamyshev, received several awards for decorating various palaces. In 1792, he helped decorate the Yekaterininsky ("Catherine") Palace at Tsarskoye Selo with colored glass, including panels of opaque white, blue, and violet glass in the bedroom of the empress. Four years later, Karamyshev was honored for decorating the Tavricheski Palace with garlands of colored glass; in 1800, he decorated the Mikhailovski Palace with mirrors and colored glass, and he also did some of the finishing of the interior.

The gamut of colored glass in the late 18th and early 19th centuries included blue (cobalt), violet (manganese), green (copper), ruby (gold), and opaque white. It was used to make cylindrical or conical forms with gilded ornament consisting of decorative bands, garlands, and medallions—a multitude of elements whose harmonious combination creates a sensation of classical simplicity and naturalness. Decoration related to that of earlier times, such as on a green glass mug, is marked by elegance and refinement. The favorite motif was a garland of small flowers in gold and green enamel (no. 15). Decoration made at the turn of the 19th century, such as those on a red decanter, are simpler and even somewhat stiff (no. 16).

The medallions, which were an indispensable part of the ornament, contain owners' monograms, which replaced the family emblems of the baroque period. Most of the monograms were made in Latin capital letters, which was only natural because the Russian aristocracy preferred to use French, and some of its members had a very poor command of their native language. Unfortunately, in some cases, the monograms are impossible to decipher. A decanter of gold ruby glass (no. 16) has the monogram "RDS" beneath a princely crown, which shows that it belonged to an as yet unidentified member of the imperial family. A covered goblet of blue glass (no. 17) has two unidentified monograms, "RR" in Latin letters in the medallion and "L.P." in Cyrillic characters in a rural landscape.

The opaque white glass made at the Imperial Glassworks was almost indistinguishable from the porcelain that it was supposed to imitate. Opaque white products included tableware, church utensils, chalices, dishes, and Easter eggs (no. 19).

The painting of both colored and colorless glass at the Imperial Glassworks was supervised by Pyotr Neupokoyev. In 1796, he was appointed master of "painting and of making up chemical paints." The factory also employed the painter Vasily Solodovnikov and eight apprentices. The masters used different design sources for their decorations. An inventory of the painting workshop in 1792 lists a large number of French prints from "Herculaneum" books (i.e., publications of wall paintings found during the excavations of Pompeii and Herculaneum) and other works devoted to similar subjects. Using these sources, the masters managed to create an inimitable form of Russian colored glass that was classical in style and personal in feeling, characteristic of the period of sentimentalism.

The making of colored glass in the second half of the 18th century was not the exclusive privilege of the Imperial Glassworks or Lomonosov's factory. Documents indicate that at least three other Russian glasshouses produced items of colored glass. For example, an inventory of 1761 states that *shtof*s of blue glass were blown at Alexei Kornilyev's factory near Tobolsk in Siberia.

A broad range of colored glass is recorded in the papers of the glassworks founded by the landowner Alexei Bakhmetiev in the villages of Nikol'skoye and Pestravka in Penza province in 1764. Two Ukrainians, Vlas and Ivan Pankov, were invited there to start production and to train local workers. Their first pupils were the brothers Pyotr and Ivan Vershinin, the landowner's serfs. They quickly learned various trades, and shortly afterward the owner said he no longer needed the services of the Ukrainian masters. By the end of the century, the factory had become so famous for its articles of colorless and colored glass that it was supplying the imperial court (no. 21). Colored glass was made by Ivan Vershinin. Most of the decorators of Bakhmetiev's glass were "goldsmiths" —that is, masters of gilding. Fortunately, several ornamental vases for flowers of blue and violet glass painted in gold and silver have survived in a number of collections. Besides garlands and butterflies, these objects bear the following inscription in gold:

"Made in 1789 at Bakhmetiev's crystal factory in Penza province, in the district of Gorodishche, at the village of Nikol'skoye on the Vyrgan River." The year should be taken as the beginning of the production of colored glass at Bakhmetiev's glasshouse, a conclusion which helps us date other items made there. Unlike the somewhat stiff products of the Imperial Glassworks, paintings on Bakhmetiev's glass are marked by a freshness of execution. A dish for serving Easter bread, decorated with the Last Supper, is a rare example of enameled opaque white glass from the Bakhmetiev factory (no. 20).

The master of that factory, Alexander Vershinin, won well-deserved fame. He is known both as a painter and as a designer of ornaments and forms. He taught at the school of masters at the glassworks, visited St. Petersburg, and went to see other factories. In 1795, he made a service for Grand Duke Alexander Pavlovich, who became Emperor Alexander I. The suggestion of S. M. Shevchenko, curator of the factory's museum, that the violet wineglass with the monogram "A.R." (no. 22) at the Historical Museum is part of this service, has much to recommend it. The decoration of this glass differs noticeably from those of the Imperial Glassworks both in the manner of execution and in the choice of motifs. A wreath of stylized oak leaves under the rim is repeated on later Bakhmetiev products. The field of the ornamental border is filled with a pattern of dots.

Colored glass was also made at Count Fyodor Orlov's glassworks in the village of Milyutino in Kaluga province. Orlov was one of five brothers who participated in the coup d'état that brought Catherine II to the throne in 1762. His glasshouse is mentioned for the first time in the registers of the College of Manufactories in 1797. These registers contain a description of its buildings and products. In size, it was exceeded only by the Imperial Glassworks in St. Petersburg and Akim Maltsov's factory in Gus. It produced dishes of bottle-green, colorless, and colored glass that was polished, engraved, and painted. Orlov was a well-known Anglophile, and this was reflected in his glasshouse's output: bottles "in the English manner," "English beer tumblers," and the use of "English" patterns of stem faceting, filigree stems, and painting.

These brief descriptions make it possible to visualize the factory's products and English patterns—and to define some of the terms used at Russian glasshouses in the 18th century. For example, English engraving meant large engraved flowers, while English "daubing" was painting in white enamel on colorless and colored glass of the Beilby type. This enables us to attribute to Orlov's glassworks some items of colorless and colored glasses with white enameled paintings. One of these objects is a vodka bottle of blue glass decorated on one side with an eagle and the monogram of Czar Paul I (no. 23). Similar vodka bottles of blue and violet glass in the collection of the Historical Museum bear heraldic devices and engraved "English" decoration—that is, large tulips or carnations. A cup with a saucer of colorless glass with garlands painted in white enamel (no. 24) evidently is also a product of Orlov's factory. The painting reproduces garlands characteristic of early neo-classicism in a motif that is widely known in gilding and silvering on the products of the Imperial and Bakhmetiev glassworks. However, in this case, the painting is rather bold and schematic. The combination of thin, colorless glass and white enamel creates a look of modest elegance.

Filigree items—beakers and wineglasses on filigree stems of opaque white, blue, and ruby glass—were produced at the Imperial and Orlov glasshouses. Much less common are filigree objects in the manner of Venetian glass of the 16th and 17th centuries. Clearly, the maker of the decanter in the Historical Museum (no. 25) did not surpass Venetian and European masters in his filigree skills, but the fact that he turned to this rich heritage is significant. Such a trait is characteristic of the neo-classical period, which was inspired by the ideas and motifs of Greco-Roman and Renaissance art. Remarkably, the filigree decanter was intended to hold four liquors at the same time. This idea became widespread at the start of the 1800s. During that century, many Russian glassworks resumed the production of decanters for four and even six beverages. Inscriptions were sometimes used to identify the wines contained in a decanter. The Historical Museum's decanter bears four gilt medallions, each bearing the monogram "S.D." beneath a crown.

The trends in Russian glass design at the end of the 18th century continued to develop until 1820, coexisting with new artistic discoveries that considerably changed the makeup of 19th-century Russian glass. The Imperial Glassworks remained the leader in all technical and artistic innovations. It was a creative laboratory in which the best works (in terms of style) were made. Russia's provincial glasshouses were conservative, and they accepted the new somewhat belatedly. However, having mastered an artistic idea and adapted it to their technical capabilities, they remained loyal to it for a long time.

The "Orlov" service made at the Imperial Glassworks (no. 26) is an example of how neo-classical glass developed in the early 19th century. This is the earliest surviving Russian service. In the second half of the 18th century, new ideas emerged for setting the table with glass: various types of decanters, beakers, wineglasses, sugar bowls, and cruets. These were joined into ensembles by adjusting their sizes, forms, and methods of ornamentation. The items in the Orlov service are of thin, well-refined colorless glass. They are decorated in gold with delicate neo-classical acanthus leaves, which emphasize the form. The design of the service includes elements that were widely used in the 18th century. Every piece has the monogram "AO" under a nobleman's crown, revealing the owner's identity: Alexei Orlov, major general, commander of the Cossack Regiment of the Life Guard.

Items made by the outstanding master of Bakhmetiev's factory, Alexander Vershinin, look back to the 18th century. Tumblers with double walls brought him a good deal of popularity in the early 1800s. Between the walls, he placed rural landscapes made of paper, straw, moss, and grass. Other masters may have worked in the same style. One example of this glass is a tumbler (no. 27) in the collection of the Historical Museum. This is somewhat different from Vershinin's signed works in its heavier form and compressed space. However, the geometric ornament repeats the pattern on a tumbler decorated by Vershinin in 1802, in the collection of the museum at the glassworks.

The 17th and 18th centuries were marked by the emergence and rapid development of glassmaking in Russia. During that time, the leading glassmaking centers—centers that continue today—were established. The output of the glasshouses increased considerably. While the first glassworks in Russia employed just six to eight craftsmen, the Imperial Glassworks had 334 at the end of the 18th century. Moreover, the problem of finding skilled Russian workers had been solved. In the 17th and early 18th centuries, not a single glasshouse could manage without foreign masters; by the middle of the 18th century, they were no longer needed because Russian craftsmen had become proficient in all the fine points of the trade. Foreign masters, for example, took no part in the making of colored glass. The results in the artistic field were also fruitful. Having accepted the ideas of "glass in the Venetian style" and, later, Bohemian engraved glass, the Russian glassmaking school developed its own version of Baroque glass. However, it attained full artistic independence only in the second half of the 18th century. The Russian glass of the classical period demonstrates a wealth of technical methods, high skill in execution, and an inimitable style, poised for the greatness that would come in the 19th century.

Russian Glass in the 19th and Early 20th Centuries

Tamara Malinina

IN THE EARLY 19TH CENTURY, Russia's glass industry expanded rapidly. A government decree banned the import of foreign glass, while the founding of glassworks was encouraged. The huge domestic market demanded glassware. In 1813, there were 146 glasshouses located in 27 provinces. (Fourteen of them were near St. Petersburg.) By 1865, there were 188 glassworks, which employed 6,700 workers. The total annual output was worth four million silver rubles. Most of the factories produced glass containers, mirrors, sheet glass, and dishes, and only a few of them made high quality glass.

The Imperial Glassworks in St. Petersburg was still the leading factory, providing unique glass objects to decorate the interiors of the palaces owned by the imperial family and urban aristocrats. Among the particularly well-known private glasshouses were those established by members of old noble families: the Nikol'skoye Crystal Works owned by Bakhmetiev and Obolensky in Penza province and Orlov's factory at Milyutino.

The largest private glassworks, annually producing goods worth more than 100,000 rubles in the middle of the 19th century, were those in Gus' Khrustal'nyy and Dyat'kovo, owned by the Maltsov family. These industrialists controlled more than one fifth of Russia's entire glass and crystal production.

The glasshouse owned by Major General S. I. Maltsov was located in the woods of Oryol province. It employed 820 workers, including 90 masters and 387 grinders. The Gus crystal works in Vladimir province employed about 500 workers. Other 19th-century producers of quality glass were the glassworks owned by Zinovyev, Yemel'yanovka, Zalivskaya, the Gerdlichka brothers, and Bolotino.

Russian glasshouses employed both domestic and imported raw materials. Since nearly all of them used wood for fuel, they were located in forests. Their owners participated in numerous artistic initiatives. They used their money to found museums, to purchase sample products from Western firms, and to send Russian specialists to study glassmaking in foreign countries. They also assisted in organizing Russian industrial exhibitions, the first of which was held in 1829. These competitions, which involved products from many glassworks, stimulated the raising of technical and artistic levels. In the 1850s, Russian glasshouses began to display their products at international exhibitions. Private factories employed extremely talented Russian masters who, working far from the foreign influences at St. Petersburg, developed a national school of glassmaking under the influence of traditional folk art. A major role in boosting production was played by the *Journal of Manufactories and Trade (Zhurnal Manufaktur i Torgovli)*, which was published in the first half of the 19th century and included experienced specialists among its contributors.

A different trend was represented by the state-owned Imperial Glassworks, which employed western European specialists and the best of the capital's architects, painters, and sculptors. Contemporaries noted that products of this factory "in the wealth and finesse of finishing and the luxury of artistic ornamentation are on a par with the works of the first-class enterprises of the same industry in Europe. Paintings are marked by good taste and splendid artistry. The perfection and finesse of glass, especially of bright colored glass, are also noteworthy. The making of colored glass has been raised to such a high degree of perfection that it is possible to obtain all kinds of tints of colors."

A number of reforms, instigated in 1803 by the Secretary of the Russian Cabinet, D. A. Gur'yev, helped to institutionalize many of the glassworks' traditions. The goal was to improve the organization of production. A drive for higher quality was launched, and masters and experienced workers were encouraged to stay at the factory for a long time.

The supply of technical facilities and raw materials at St. Petersburg was unmatched among the private glasshouses. Stone buildings, steam engines, fuel from local estates, and raw materials from Britain made it possible to create a solid basis for a state-owned enterprise. Concern for personnel training was no less important. From the age of five or six, workers' children studied general educational subjects and the fundamentals of technical and other drawing at the factory school. The most talented graduates continued their studies for another six years at the Military School of Mines, one of the best technical schools in St. Petersburg. Masters with records of long service were sent abroad to study with Europe's leading glassmakers. There was a statute on the division of masters into classes, in keeping with the table of ranks. As a result, after a long period of service at the Imperial Glassworks (sometimes up to 40 years), a master could hope for promotion from the class of serfs to the nobility.

When speaking about personnel at the Imperial Glassworks, it is necessary to make special mention of the organizers of production. In addition to the manager, D. A. Gur'yev, two inspectors played a major role at the factory in the first quarter of the 19th century. They were S. I. Komarov, in charge of economic management, and Ye. F. Karamyshev, in charge of the crafts. Together with such masters as Levashev, Neupokoyev, Krupenin, and Nikanov, they directed research and production—and to a considerable extent, its artistic activity as well. The quality of the factory's products was brought to a high level by the cutters and engravers Veselkin, Frolov, and Yevdokimov, and by the painters Neupokoyev, Nikiforov, Novikova, and Ryadov.

Because the interiors of the many palaces built in St. Petersburg in the early 19th century were decorated with exquisite furniture, lamps. and vases, the Imperial Glassworks needed designers of works of art. The Cabinet therefore decided to introduce the post of designer and to invite Thomas de Thomon to fill it. De Thomon was a famous architect and a remarkable graphic artist. Many architectural masterpieces that beautified St. Petersburg in the early 1800s were built to his design. Thus, his invitation characterizes

3. Tripod Vase.
Blown, cut,
gilded bronze mounts.
Designed by
Thomas de Thomon,
Imperial Glassworks,
St. Petersburg, 1807.
H. 165 cm.
State Hermitage Museum,
Leningrad.

the Imperial Glassworks as one of the art industry's progressive enterprises. In view of the specifics of production, the management even found it necessary to give de Thomon a "drawing test" before awarding him the job. He stayed at the factory from 1804 to 1813.

On July 31, 1814, there was a petition from another eminent architect of St. Petersburg, K. I. Rossi, with a directive issued by the cabinet manager Gur'yev, who "deigned to suggest verbally that architect Rossi should be engaged in place of the deceased architect Thomon, who, as is known, was employed at the Imperial Glass and China Works for making drawings of various things." It is known that Rossi received the position of architect in 1806, when Gur'yev asked him to make various drawings for the glasshouse and other manufactories. In 1819, a petition from Rossi stated, "Having no time, in view of various commissions from the Imperial Glassworks, to make drawings and other inventions necessary for it, I hereby ask to be dismissed from the latter and to stop paying me the salary from the sums of the works."

These outstanding architects were succeeded by I. A. Ivanov, who had served with the Cabinet from 1806 "for drawing various pictures and for copying drawings." He began to work at the Imperial Glassworks in 1815. In reply to an inquiry from the Cabinet in 1830, the factory said that "Ivanov makes drawings of items chiefly made for presentation to the emperor; his items are marked by the fineness of form and deserve every praise."

Thus, what has been said about the history of the Imperial Glassworks in the first quarter of the 19th century makes it possible to conclude that it was the leading center of glassmaking in Russia, with well-organized production and a carefully planned system of training highly skilled personnel. The great demands placed on its output reflected the particular responsibility of its managers for the work entrusted to them. They were always under the patronage of the Cabinet, receiving orders for glass objects from members of the imperial family. Christmas, Easter, and New Year's presents; gifts to mark patron saints' days, the making of dowries, and additions to the services of palaces, country houses, and yachts; preparing exhibits for international fairs—these were just some of the factory's products and duties.

The management of the glassworks changed many times during the 19th century. In 1829, the manager Komarov was replaced by Pensky; in 1832, the post was given to Ivanov, who was in turn replaced by Demin in 1848. Derevitsky, who directed the factory in 1856, was replaced by Knipper 10 years later.

There were families of Russian glassmakers at the Imperial Glassworks in the first third of the 19th century. These included the Karamyshevs, the Levashevs, and the Neupoko-yevs, and they were the backbone of the factory's skilled personnel. They continued to work actively in the subsequent period, and they were joined by their children and pupils.

The surviving map of the Imperial Glassworks shows that it was located on the left bank of the Neva River, on land rented from the Alexander Nevsky monastery. The factory occupied some 600 acres. In addition to the glassworks itself, there were state-

**4. Vase with
Nereid-shaped Handles.**
Blown, cut,
gilded bronze mounts.
Designed by Ivan Ivanov,
Imperial Glassworks,
St. Petersburg, 1841–1842.
H. 130 cm.
State Hermitage Museum,
Leningrad.

owned houses containing apartments that were leased to the workers. The factory also permitted its employees to build their own houses on the grounds, and it supplied them with credit. The property included a church, a school, a factory shop, and an inn. The sick were treated at the hospital, whose upkeep was financed by deducting one percent from the wages, according to the 1853 staff registers.

In 1833, the Imperial Glassworks had both stone and wooden buildings. The "dish pavilion," the "mirror pavilion," and the workshop for the treatment of plate glass by a "machine" required fireproof quarters, so they were housed in stone buildings. Wooden structures were built for the "cutting and faceting workshop," the "painting shop," the warehouse for raw materials, the "pottery," the "potassium carbonate pavilion," the "plaster of Paris workshop," and the "workshop for the hand working of plate glass." Later, when these buildings were repaired and rebuilt, the wooden structures were replaced in stone. A pipeline was laid in 1857 to supply water from the Neva to the steam engine in the cutting and engraving workshop. Another steam engine was made for the factory by Thomson's Neva Foundry and Mechanical Engineering Plant.

The survival of the glassworks depended on regular subsidies. The Secretary of the Cabinet, L. Perovsky, observed in 1853: "The experience of many years has shown that the china and glass works are unable to maintain themselves with their own money. Such enterprises as the Imperial China and Glass Works produce almost exclusively luxury items and therefore should be supported by government funds." Nevertheless, a small portion of the glasshouse's products was put on sale in various shops in St. Petersburg and Moscow. If there was an opportunity to sell glass objects retail, it was never missed. Besides, with the Cabinet's permission, the factory also made some items on private orders, chiefly from the metropolitan aristocracy.

The work was done by people "attached to the Glassworks and constituting the property of the Czar. The above-mentioned people have a special status, namely, they are exempt from taxation and military service. They are obliged to work at the glassworks an indefinite number of years and are dismissed only on the grounds of advanced age, ill health, and weakness." Masters of average skills received annual wages of 250 to 350 rubles, apprentices got 120 to 250 rubles, and workmen earned 80 to 120 rubles.

The reform of 1861, which abolished serfdom, affected all Russian glassworks, both private and state-owned, where serfs made up the bulk of the work force. Many of these factories closed down. In 1862, the Imperial Glassworks was to be sold by auction. To save the plant, several steps were taken. Some personnel cuts were made by dismissing low-skilled workers. The glassworks, which had employed 149 people in 1861, reduced that number to 115 in 1863. In addition, the factory school was closed. Nevertheless, the public sale of the plant was canceled on August 25, 1866. It was decided to continue glassmaking on a reduced scale. To this end, a grant of 5,000 rubles was given to the factory from Cabinet funds. The glasshouse was also to receive 6,000 rubles annually, 15,000 rubles for its products presented to the imperial court, and 8,000 rubles for the tesserae needed for the mosaics factory. The glassworks gained the exclusive right of repairing crystal services, and it also received private orders and permission to sell its products to private individuals. By the end of the 1860s, the factory's financial position had been strengthened, and the number of workers reached 250.

After the 1861 reform, the management of the glasshouse carried out a number of measures intended to improve working and living conditions, to encourage experienced workers to stay on, and to increase the quality of output. Besides providing its employees with housing, the factory based their pay on the level of their training and skills. Most of the workers were on salary, while the top masters were paid on a piece rate. Salaries reached 300 to 500 silver rubles a year, while the heads of the workshops received up to 1,500 rubles.

Making glass required a streamlined operation. All stages of production were equally important, from the correct composition of the batch to a steady hand to finish the engraving.

The "dish pavilion," where glass was melted, had two glassmaking furnaces of eight pots each. A furnace was used continuously for 18 months, and then it was shut down for repairs. A complete overhaul occurred after four years of use. Glass was melted in one furnace, which had six covered and two open pots. It took 18 to 24 hours to prepare the glass in a covered pot and 12 to 18 hours when using an open pot.

In the 1830s and 1840s, the master in charge of the composition of the glass batch was D. K. Semyonov. He had worked at the glasshouse for about 40 years and received one of the highest salaries. In 1830, Semyonov was sent to Paris to present works of art from the factory to the French king as gifts from Czar Nicholas I and to "review French factories and notice everything that is the best therein." He was replaced by V. Zhirnov in 1857, and in 1868 there were two masters, A. Pavlov and M. Martynov, at the dish pavilion. Objects were made there by blowing or casting the glass in wooden, metal, or earthenware molds. (The same techniques are used in Soviet glassworks today.) Martynov and an apprentice, Ilya Bogachev, were among the most talented workmen at the factory. They fashioned unique works of art, and they were entrusted with making "the largest and most difficult things." Documents show that the masters Alexander Nikitin and Mikhail Zubov were also excellent glassmaking specialists.

Beginning in 1852, a screw press was used in molding some of the objects. It was operated by the mechanic Scarp. At private glassworks, press operators were called "pourers" because they poured glass under the press.

Many types of colored glass were melted in the furnaces of the dish pavilion: white (colored with arsenic and tin or antimony), blue (cobalt), green (copper or chrome), yellow (antimony with lead), red (copper oxide and manganese), violet (manganese), rose or gold ruby, and aventurine. These technical achievements were due to the activity of chemists at the factory.

As one of the advanced industrial enterprises of its day, the glassworks followed every innovation in European glassmaking. The management looked for experienced chemists both inside and outside Russia. Dmitry Kartsev, the factory's chemist after 1832, had studied at Moscow University and taken part in the military campaigns in Europe in 1814. His petition, preserved in the factory's files, shows that while he was in Paris, he had studied "at all schools linked with chemistry in one way or another." Under his direction, the St. Petersburg glasshouse started to produce "lithyalin" and "hyalith" glass (no. 44). "Lithyalin" glass, invented by Egermann at the Nový Bor factory in Bohemia, imitated marble or colored jasper. Kartsev also designed glass objects. Unfortunately, he left St. Petersburg in 1834 to move to Moscow, thus compelling the managers to renew their search for experienced technicians. In the same year, Prince Nicholas Gruzinsky took a job at the glassworks as an "official for special missions in charge of arts and crafts."

In 1847, the glasshouse signed a contract with the French chemist Marceau, who pledged "to train two capable apprentices within five years in everything related to the manufacture of glass so that they could replace him at the enterprise in every respect." The contract shows that Marceau was an outstanding specialist in handling every stage of the manufacturing process. The glassworks, which wanted to improve output quality and reduce production costs, went to great expense to hire him. (He received 50 percent more than an experienced master.) The management's goal was not to depend on foreign specialists, but to train local skilled personnel. Invitations were extended to two industrial engineers, G. Serebryannikov and A. Khovansky, who had graduated from the St. Petersburg Institute of Technology. In addition to training under the guidance of a foreign specialist, they were supposed to learn practical skills from experienced masters. When Khovansky, who considered his activity useless, left the glassworks, the management invited two more industrial engineers, E. Miller and P. Mikhailov. The latter devoted 20 years to the glasshouse. S. Petukhov, another talented industrial engineer, worked at the factory from 1869 to 1892. He was a friend of the outstanding Russian chemist D. Mendeleyev, who wrote a preface to Petukhov's book *Glassmaking*, in which the Imperial Glassworks' chemist summed up his activities.

Two Italian mosaic chemists, the brothers Justinian and Leopold Bonafede, came to Russia from Rome in 1852. They both worked as chief chemists at the St. Petersburg glasshouse, Justinian from 1857 to 1866 and Leopold until 1878. Their activities are associated with the founding of the mosaic department at the Imperial Glassworks. The making of mosaics was required for the finishing work in St. Isaac's Cathedral and other churches. By early 1862, the shop of the mosaic department had up to 20,000 tesserae of all colors, a collection not inferior to that of the Vatican.

As in preceding years, the "cutting and faceting workshop" and the painting workshop determined the artistic level of St. Petersburg glassmaking. The "cutting and faceting workshop" employed especially experienced professionals because cutting required a knowledge of the possibilities of the material, technique, an artistic talent for "drawing" on glass, and an understanding of how to handle the wheel. Faceting also required a particular knack. Workmen had to know how to operate special steam engines. The level of their training was regulated by the statute of the classes of the work they performed, which said that "those who finish objects with rich ornaments are considered to be in the first class; those who treat objects not requiring such rich finishing are in the second class. They can also engage in ordinary engraving. Those who were moved up from apprentices to workmen and can do only ordinary engraving belong to the third class."

Documents show that the shop's best workers in the mid-1800s included the commissioner Vasily Voronov and the masters Alexander Voronov (1792–1830), Lev Karamyshev (1802–?), Stepan Ratmanov (1804–1859), and Ilya Moryakhin (1804–1844). The senior master of the shop in 1868 was Nikolai Sobolev, who worked with the masters Nikitin, Zubov, Glazunov, and Seryakov. Besides the Russian names, there is mention of a Prussian, the master engraver J. Gube, who trained the apprentices Gavrila Glazunov, Gavrila Muzhikov, and Konstantin Plakhov during his stay at the factory (1839–1852).

Between 1840 and 1880, the St. Petersburg Glassworks made a large number of services for members of the imperial court. These services were intended as parts of dowries. As a rule, crystal objects were decorated with the customers' emblems and monograms, so it became necessary to hire a monogram cutter, the "freelance master" Gerasim Sergeyev.

Even in the early 1800s, the painting workshop was in a somewhat special and privileged position. The management regularly supplied it with magazines, other illustrated publications, and information about new exhibitions and the main trends in the foreign glassmaking industry. All of the glasshouse's promising new workers who could draw were trained at a school under the direction of experienced teachers. Some of the artists attended drawing classes at the Academy of Arts on their own initiative and with the management's permission. In the late 19th century, such artists also attended classes at the Baron Stieglitz School of Technical Drawing in St. Petersburg, which trained specialists for the art industry. ·

Frequent trips abroad, both to visit exhibitions and on diplomatic missions to deliver gifts, enabled artists to study the organization of the glass industry in Bohemia, France, and Britain. These specialists were instructed to purchase specimen products from foreign glasshouses for the factory's own museum. With the exception of its designer, the Imperial Glassworks had no professional artist on the staff until 1848. Designs were made by the chemists (Kartsev and the Bonafede brothers) or by the masters of the painting workshop, who determined both subject matter and style. These were sometimes borrowed from the literature coming to the glassworks. The *Catalog of Books, Publications, and Drawings of the Imperial China Works*, numbered 568 titles and contained the main sources on the history of Italian, Greek, French, German, Japanese, and Chinese culture that were issued in the second half of the 19th century.

Among the glasshouse's prominent painters were the master Vasily Kitayev, who worked at the factory from 1790 to 1841; E. Filippov, a master from 1838 to 1848; and Ivan

Karamyshev, who was known for his high professional qualities and was appointed senior master in 1858. Karamyshev, who directed the painting shop until his death, had no artistic education. However, his successor, Ivan Murinov, had attended drawing classes at the Imperial Academy of Arts. He was noticed by the chief chemist Bonafede, who supervised his work. The manager of the glasshouse noted Murinov's success when he compared the production and sales of painted glass objects before and during Murinov's tenure. In addition to the masters, the painting shop had seven apprentices, five workmen or artisans, and two general workers.

The French painter Brianchon was invited to the St. Petersburg glasshouse in 1848. Evidently, he was a relative of the Parisian glass factory owner Brianchon, who supplied raw materials to the Imperial Glassworks. The St. Petersburg factory's archives state that Brianchon installed new muffle furnaces "similar to those at Sèvres" for firing enameled objects. These furnaces improved the quality of the enameling. That the French master also knew the secrets of producing the enamels themselves is indicated by the papers outlining his role in training Russian industrial engineers. When the Berlin painter Wurtzel offered in 1853 to improve glass painting at the Imperial Glassworks, the management declined, noting that instead of the three or four tones used by Wurtzel, the factory employed 30 to 40. This fact underscores the glasshouse's high standard of enameling. Its technical facilities made possible a number of original designs produced by such outstanding architects as A. Brüllov, O. Monferran, I. Monighetti, V. Hartmann, and H. Krakau. In the mid-1800s, architects were invited to design glass objects only periodically; in the preceding period, they had been members of the factory's staff.

The Imperial Glassworks, like many other Russian enterprises involved with the applied arts, took part in international exhibitions. At the 1862 London world's fair, the glasshouse received a medal "for the excellent finish of elegant vases," while the collection of tesserae (420 types) attracted special attention and was presented to the British Museum. The factory's exhibits had been designed by the architects Bosse, Monighetti, and Krakau. Among the works that won awards at the 1867 Paris exhibition were those by the chief chemist Leopold Bonafede, the industrial engineer P. Mikhailov, the laboratory technician Alexander Pavlov, and the masters Ivan Karamyshev, Nikolai Sobolev, Andrei Martynov, Alexander Nikitin, and Ivan Murinov. The Office of the Department of State-Owned Works noted that these "items were beyond compare."

Bonafede, who also received the Order of the Legion of Honor from the French government, represented the Imperial Glassworks again at the Vienna world's fair in 1873. Glass objects designed by Monighetti, Bruni, and Prince Gagarin were featured at that exposition. An international jury accorded these displays honorary certificates, which were "the highest awards at the exhibition."

Although the Imperial Glassworks was an obvious success, the question of whether it was expedient to keep it among the state-owned enterprises arose again in the 1880s: "There was a time when it was intended to turn it over to the Academy of Arts together with the Imperial China Works. However, the Academy did not find it possible to assume the management of it." It was then decided to join the china and glass works, the two oldest state-owned companies in St. Petersburg, and they merged in June 1890. Some of the production facilities of the glasshouse were moved to the grounds of the china works, and the joint enterprise was named the Imperial China and Glass Works. After the merger, Ivan Murinov was in charge of design from 1894 to 1901.

Among the private glasshouses, the Nikol'skoye Crystal Works should be singled out for the quality of its products. It belonged to the aristocratic family of the Bakhmetievs. Contemporaries described its products as follows: "The Nikol'skoye Crystal Works . . . chiefly manufactures such items where special attention is paid to surface finishing and ornamentation. The collection submitted by the works [to the 1862 London exhibition] was very diversified, consisting of such different items as vases, bowls, beakers, decanters, tumblers, candlesticks, etc., of faceted and ground gilded glass decorated with patterns, paintings, and bronze."

The Nikol'skoye Crystal Works was owned by three generations of Bakhmetievs until 1884. After the death of the last owner, Anna Bakhmetieva, the crystal and glass factories passed to her grandnephew Prince A. Obolensky. Throughout its long history, the Nikol'skoye-Bakhmetiev Crystal Works participated in all the major Russian industrial exhibitions. In 1836, it received the right to stamp its products with the national emblem. Later, this award, given to the best factories in Russia, was conferred at the exhibitions held in Moscow (1839, 1861, and 1865) and Nizhni Novgorod (1896). The factory was also awarded a gold medal at the 1900 Paris world's fair.

The company was widely known for its crystal objects. Their production had been started by the owner N. A. Bakhmetiev. Lead crystal, which had been perfected by the English chemist George Ravenscroft in the late 17th century, became extremely popular in Europe in the early 1800s. Many European courts, including that of St. Petersburg, bought English crystal items because of their elegant forms, the purity of the glass, and their sparkling facets.

English glassmakers had developed various types of cutting. The use and combination of different patterns made it possible, in producing large numbers of items, to alter the ornamentation on objects that had similar shapes. As early as 1800, Bakhmetiev was the first Russian factory owner to pay attention to this feature of English cut glass, which permitted the production of quality items while keeping manufacturing costs low. As a result, his factory attempted to make products "in the English manner."

On more than one occasion, Bakhmetiev appealed to the College of Manufactories to ban the import of crystal in order "to revive this branch of industry and to make it flourish." He sent products from his factory to the minister of the interior, Count Kochubey, to compare them with imported crystal. These samples were approved by Czar Alexander I.

Alexander Vershinin, the son of the founder of the Vershinin dynasty, was in charge of all technical and artistic work at the factory from 1795 to 1822. He had studied glassmaking at the Imperial Glassworks in St. Petersburg, and for this reason the products of the two factories in the first third of the 19th century are so close, both in quality and in the manner of execution, that experts cannot always tell them apart.

In 1836, Alexei Bakhmetiev, a high-ranking official of the imperial court, became the owner of the crystal factory in Nikol'skoye. Bakhmetiev, who brought the business to the "summit of flourishing," was well educated. For a long time, he had lived in Leipzig and Paris, where he studied glassmaking techniques and even took factory jobs as an ordinary worker, "sparing neither money nor effort" to improve the operation of his glassworks.

The owners of the Nikol'skoye-Bakhmetiev Crystal Works wanted to make luxury glass in rather large numbers, so they employed more cutters and grinders than other factories. In 1841, there were 124 workers in the cutting and grinding shop. The "gilding" or painting shop had 18 masters, 10 apprentices, and three workmen. The "bronze factory" employed 25 masters, nine apprentices, and four workmen.

By comparison, the Imperial Glassworks had six masters, 18 apprentices, 33 workmen, 13 pupils, and eight general workers in its cutting and grinding shop—that is, almost 50 fewer people than at Nikol'skoye. The position of the latter factory as a private enterprise obliged its owners to look for new ways to improve production, reduce costs, and develop new products that would be in demand. The Bakhmetievs had to deal with the most difficult problem in the applied arts: the conflict between mass production and quality. The Imperial Glassworks, being a state-owned enterprise, had practically never confronted the issue.

In the 1830s and 1840s, masters at the Penza factory, looking for new types of ornament, turned to folk art, and adapted traditional wood-carving motifs.

After the death of Alexei Bakhmetiev, his widow tried to run the business at its former level. However, wishing to reduce production costs, she made use of inferior materials, and this affected the quality of the products.

The last owner of this private crystal factory, Prince A. Obolensky, expanded production considerably, improved equipment in keeping with the latest technological standards, and succeeded in hiring skillful technical personnel. Improvements in the railway system provided a major impetus to the factory's expansion, assisting sales and the speedy delivery of raw materials. Price lists, which played an important role in advertising products, offered a wide range of glass objects to wholesale and retail customers. According to a 1911 price list, the factory made more than 10 types of services, each numbering more than 130 items. A customer could order a pattern of cutting or engraving to suit his taste and budget. Forty-five varieties of decoration were offered. Traders received products from warehouses in Moscow, Penza, and Samara. These goods were sold chiefly in the Moscow and Volga regions, western Siberia, and Iran.

The products of the Nikol'skoye factory are characterized by a variety of techniques and types. Masters were able to produce glass in a broad range of colors, including

5. Vase in Five Parts.
Blown, overlaid, cut,
enameled, gilded.
Enameled by
Pavel Volkov,
Mikhail Orlov's
glassworks,
Milyutino, Kaluga
province, 1839.
H. 80.5 cm.
State Russian
Museum, Leningrad.

marble and opal. They made glass objects with Venetian trailing. They also interpreted the styles of western European and Russian glassmakers in their own way, and they made use of their own traditions in developing new glass forms and types of decoration.

Mikhail Orlov's glassworks in Kaluga province occupies a special place among the industry's private enterprises. As a member of the underground Union of Prosperity, Orlov took part in the anti-government plot of December 14, 1825. Banished to his estate, he turned to chemistry and running the glass factory he inherited from his father. Orlov was particulary interested in painting on glass with transparent enamels, and he set up an experimental workshop for this purpose. At the First Industrial Exhibition in 1829, Orlov's glasshouse displayed "gilded colored glass and many-faceted crystal." The factory showed more enameled objects at the 1835 exhibition. Among its masterpieces are a pair of vases made in 1839 (now in the collection of the State Russian Museum). These vases were painted with many colors of transparent enamel by the talented master Volkov. After Orlov's death in 1842, the glassworks was sold to Zalivskaya, and it had ceased to exist by 1862.

The Maltsov family owned a veritable glassmaking empire in the 19th century. In 1809, they operated 12 glass and crystal factories in Vladimir province alone. Among these enterprises was the widely known Gus Crystal Works. In 1814, Ivan Maltsov sold that factory to his brother Sergei, and Sergei's son, Ivan, owned it from 1823 to 1880. Sergei Maltsov, who also operated the Dyat'kovo Crystal Works in Bryansk province, was called the "crystal king." As a member of the College of Foreign Affairs, he often traveled abroad and studied the work of foreign industrialists. A letter written by Maltsov to S. A. Sobolevsky (a friend of the poet Alexander Pushkin) reports on an 1835 visit to Bohemia. "Bohemian factories are very poor," he wrote. Maltsov factories, on the other hand, did things in a big way, Russian style. In 1859, the Dyat'kovo glasshouse produced about 2.5 million glass objects, while Gus turned out about 1.5 million quality crystal items.

In 1857, the Gus Crystal Works was allowed to put the national emblem on its products "for the purity and artistry of its crystal." By the end of the century, the Maltsovs' glass had been acclaimed not only in Russia but also in other countries. Glassmakers from Gus' Khrustal'nyy won a bronze medal at the 1893 world's fair in Chicago, and they were awarded the top prize at the Paris exhibition in 1900.

Masters at the Maltsov factory concentrated solely on production. A workday lasted 12 hours. The blowers' work was particularly demanding, and few masters lived to the age of 40. Child labor was also used. All of the masters at Ivan Maltsov's factories were Russians, and many of them formed glassmakers' dynasties. The chief technicians and managers were often former peasants from neighboring villages.

One of the last owners, Yuri Nechayev-Maltsov, was a well-known patron of the arts. He donated money to build the Fine Arts Museum (today the Pushkin State Fine Arts Museum) in Moscow in 1900.

To complete this survey of glass production in Russia in the 19th and early 20th centuries, several more glassworks must be mentioned. One of them, the Krugov Crystal Works, was founded by Prince Alexander Menshikov in the province of Moscow in 1835. It manufactured a variety of dishes, chandeliers, vases, girandoles, candlesticks, lamp globes, lampshades, and bottles. Prince Menshikov was the great-grandson of a close associate of Peter the Great, the founder of St. Petersburg. His great-grandfather, whose name was also Prince Alexander Menshikov, owned a glasshouse in Yamburg in the first third of the 18th century. The Krugov factory, which had four glass-melting furnaces and 104 grinding machines, employed 240 workers.

V. A. Olsufyev owned a large crystal works in Smolensk province. In 1859, the factory's 325 workers produced crystal dishes worth 100,000 rubles.

In the late 1800s and early 1900s, Russia became a major glassmaking country, boasting 277 glassworks with an annual turnover of more than 50 million silver rubles. These factories, situated in 54 provinces and regions, employed 60,000 workers. Beginning in 1906, glasshouse owners held regular congresses in Moscow to discuss urgent issues facing their industry. They also published the results of their meetings.

6. Candelabrum.
Blown, cut, gilded
bronze mounts.
Designed by
V. P. Stasov,
Imperial Glassworks,
St. Petersburg,
mid-19th century.
H. 320 cm.
State Hermitage Museum,
Leningrad.

Russian glass objects of the 19th and early 20th centuries reflect important historical and cultural events in that country. They also vividly demonstrate the diversity of forms, techniques, and methods of operation employed in Russian glassworks. Like other works of art, these glass objects show the evolution from high classicism to the modernist style; however, they also have specific features of their own.

A string of splendid architectural ensembles went up in St. Petersburg and its environs in the early 19th century. They were designed by such eminent Russian architects as K. Rossi, T. de Thomon, A. Zakharov, and A. Voronikhin. Their palaces, cathedrals, public buildings, squares, and parks continue to beautify St. Petersburg (Leningrad) and to create a remarkable harmony between architecture and the environment. Russian architects of the 19th century, like those in the preceding period, paid considerable attention to interior decoration, using furniture, tapestries, lamps, and vases to produce an integrated artistic image. Crystal floor lamps several meters high, chandeliers, and monumental decorative vases with sparkling facets and gilded bronze still adorn the classical interiors of the main rooms in the imperial family's residences.

The outstanding Russian architect A. N. Voronikhin, who created various items for interior decoration in the early 1800s, brought world fame to Russian decorative and applied art. He was also one of the first Russian architects to design lead glass (crystal) objects. Crystal was a new material in Russia in the early 19th century, and Voronikhin was the first to discover its highly decorative qualities. His works marked a new stage in glassmaking and raised this craft to the level of high art. His drawings for the Imperial China Works and for the Peterhof and Yekaterinburg faceting factories are well known, and many furniture makers and bronzers in St. Petersburg also used his designs. Unfortunately, only five of his drawings, made for the Imperial Glassworks, have survived. Of the surviving crystal objects made by Voronikhin, a washing set and a chandelier from the Pavlovsk Palace Museum enjoy world renown. Works of art made to three other designs have not yet been found. Some of these objects are ascribed to Voronikhin on the basis of historical information and stylistic analysis.

The tripod vase (no. 28) is also considered to be one of Voronikhin's works. It consists of a large bowl on a tripod made in the form of three crystal herms with bronze heads of eagles supported by bronze paws. The herms are connected by struts in the shape of bronze arrows piercing balls. The cut decoration on the bowl is also made to an original design, with a large eight-pointed star in the center. The star resembles a stylized flower, from which diamonds branch out along the edge. According to the archives of the State Hermitage, this object and a similar tripod vase were delivered to the czar's residence, the Winter Palace, in the early 1800s. These vases decorated the room of Empress Maria Feodorovna until 1829. After her death, they were kept in the palace storeroom.

In his works, Voronikhin used soft and rounded lines to reveal the plasticity of crystal, its link with the gather from which the object is blown. In the decoration of crystal, it was important for this architect to underline the sparkling of the well-polished facets with the play of the sun's rays on them. As a result, he turned to bronze only when he needed to connect the parts of a multi-component work. Voronikhin introduced a new form for Russian objects: a shallow, curved bowl. He carved an entirely new design—an eight-lobed floral star—in decorating the bowl on the tripod. His tripod vase is a masterpiece of Russian decorative and applied art. The composition and the carved decoration are remarkable for their clarity and harmony, typical of classicism.

A considerable number of monumental and decorative works were made to the designs of I. A. Ivanov, the artistic manager at the Imperial Glassworks from 1815 to 1848. He made numerous glass objects to present to members of the imperial family on holidays, to be used as diplomatic gifts, and to be shown at industrial fairs. When it became necessary to redecorate the interior of the Winter Palace after a fire in 1837, Ivanov faced the extremely difficult task of making large crystal objects. However, he had directed the development of a new technique for producing such objects as early as the

1820s. They were made of separate molded components assembled with metal fastenings. This method permitted the manufacture of vases more than two meters high. These objects were decorated with deep faceting, and the patterns were extremely diverse and original. Two exotic, monumental items, made in 1819–1822 to Ivanov's design as a gift for the Shah of Iran, were a crystal swimming pool and a bed. Both were highly praised. Ivanov was a master in a transition period, which is seen in the absence of harmony in the proportions of the tripod vase (no. 29), overcrowded with "diamond" cutting.

Crystal objects decorated with portraits of heroic military leaders and inscriptions reflecting events of the Patriotic War (1812–1814) became widely known in Russia. Their appearance among the products of the Imperial and Nikol'skoye-Bakhmetiev glassworks was due to an upsurge of patriotism among the Russian people, who had defended their independence in the war against Napoleon. These objects were made as souvenirs and presented to the veterans of the war.

One example is a covered goblet decorated with diamond cutting and a superimposed medallion of opal glass that shows Victory hovering over a map of Europe marked with the battlefields of the war (no. 30). Such items, which were first made in St. Petersburg, were imitated at the Nikol'skoye-Bakhmetiev glasshouse. The quality of the enameling was insured by the work of experienced masters and that of the court miniature painter P. E. Rockstuhl, who specialized in portraits. A serf master of the Bakhmetievs, A. P. Vershinin, had studied art in St. Petersburg, and he also achieved a considerable success in portrait painting.

The subject of valor in the Patriotic War was also reflected in a series of objects bearing portraits of war heroes painted in gold on colored glass. In making a portrait of Count Wittgenstein, the painter scrupulously followed the original produced by I. Chessky (no. 31).

A plate with an engraved allegorical composition, "Peace to Europe," is devoted to the same subject (no. 32). In keeping with the laws of classicism, it shows Russia personified by the majestic figure of a woman holding out her hand over the kneeling genius of Europe. This plate and a sulphide paperweight (no. 33) are some of many items made at the Imperial Glassworks from medallions by the well-known Russian sculptor Count F. P. Tolstoy in the late 1830s and 1840s. Between 1814 and 1834, Tolstoy produced 21 medallions reflecting milestones in the war against Napoleon. Among them are "Home Guard," "Battle of Borodino," "Liberation of Moscow," "Liberation of Berlin," "Conquest of Paris," and "Battle of Brienne." Later, the masters I. Klepikov and A. Lyalin used them as models for medals produced at the St. Petersburg mint. These very popular medallions were widely used in Russian decorative and applied art until the mid-1800s. Thanks to the skills of such engravers as Johann Gube, Muzhikov, Glazunov, and Plakhov, the Imperial Glassworks was able to produce the subjects of Tolstoy's medallions on crystal objects.

Colored glass, sometimes used in combination with colorless glass, reappeared in the products of Russia's glassworks by the late 1820s. Objects with two or three layers of glass were also popular. One major work of this type is the two-layer vase *Medici* (no. 34). It is remarkable for its noble form, its color, and the high quality of its bronze mounts. The scarlet layer is covered by colorless glass, and the object also combines the splendor of diamond cutting with rich color. Gold had been used to produce ruby glass at the Imperial Glassworks since Lomonosov's time, and this type of glass was called "gold ruby." It is possible that this vase or a copy was one of the products of the Imperial Glassworks displayed at the First Industrial Exhibition in St. Petersburg in 1829.

Products of the Imperial Glassworks in the first third of the 19th century were often set in magnificently chased gilded bronze made both by the factory's bronze shop and by St. Petersburg's best private bronze workers, who supplied the imperial court. They also made bronze fixtures for the many chandeliers that adorned the halls of St. Petersburg's and suburban palaces. A small oval vase of ruby glass with bronze handles, made in the shape of eagles, and decorated with diamond cutting, is an excellent example of the cooperation between St. Petersburg's glassmakers and bronze founders in the classical era. This vase is mounted on a high bronze pedestal (no. 35). The small vase with opalescent pink glass, mounted in ormolu and on a malachite base, is also typical of the factory's products (no. 36).

The skills of Russian masters in producing objects with three layers of glass can be seen in a decanter and stopper made of ruby, white, and green glass in the 1830s or 1840s (no. 37).

The design of Russian glass objects was greatly influenced by the banquet services made at the Imperial Glassworks for members of the imperial family in the middle of the 19th century. They showed the owners' enameled gold foil monograms encrusted within thick glass coatings. The same encrustation technique was used in decorating separate items, such as a decanter of clear crystal made in a traditional shape. Ornamented with four medallions on the body and one on the stopper, it features bright, rich colors and bunches of flowers enameled on gold foil (no. 38).

Artists at the Imperial Glassworks, who created collections of flowers and plants for the enameling shop, spent much of their time in the St. Petersburg Botanical Garden. Luxurious albums containing pictures of the world's diversified plants and animals were regularly purchased for state-owned factories.

Masters at the Dyat'kovo Crystal Works used a similar technique. An example of their work is a crystal goblet with a large encrusted ornament decorated with the coat of arms of the noble Kolokoltsov family. The ornament is also made of gold foil and enamel encased in a thick crystal coating (no. 39).

In addition to individual items, 19th-century Russian glassworks made large services. Many of these sets were made at the Imperial Glassworks throughout the 1800s for the storerooms of the imperial family's palaces and the mansions of the metropolitan aristocracy. Some names of services were "Orlov's," "Faceted," "With an Emblem," "Gothic," "In the English Manner with Cut Vine Leaves," "For Banquets," "Bakhmetiev's," "Old and New Maltsovs'," and "With a Broad Facet." Services were also produced for the imperial yachts *Derzhava* (Power), *Livadiya*, *Shtandart* (Standard), and *Czarevna* (Princess). Designs for these sets were made by I. Ivanov, the artistic manager at the Imperial Glassworks. In the 1870s, designs were produced by the architect I. A. Monighetti. Some of the services were modeled on items from other Russian and foreign glassworks.

No. 41 is part of the "Gothic" service, made at the Imperial Glassworks in the 1830s and 1840s. Its name points to a departure from the classical forms of decoration and reflects the cultural heritage of the preceding eras, in particular the Middle Ages. This set is entirely different from other glass services. Its large items—vases, decanters, and bowls—are made of colorless glass with blue and green overlays, and they are decorated with rich faceting. The small items combine colored and colorless glass. The designer of the "Gothic" service boldly upset the traditional view of the plasticity of glass, producing "thorny" objects and underlining them with the sharp edges of facets. A wineglass for Rhine wine is in the form of a medieval *Römer*, and a clear, bright green color similar to that used in medieval stained glass windows is often employed. The shape of the items in the service, combined with their cut and colored decoration, provides a romantic "Gothic" touch.

Neo-Gothic art was one of the manifestations of historicism. Items of decorative and applied art with a Gothic look appeared in classical interiors as early as the 1820s. Items were made in this style at the Imperial Glassworks and many private glasshouses. A Gothic image was particularly successful when it combined medieval decoration and vertical lines. This combination is clearly seen in the items of the "Gothic" service.

Interest in the history and culture of different countries, which emerged in the 1830s, inspired a keen attention to the traits and details of historical styles. Artists of the 19th century wanted to master the experience of the past and to use its designs to create works imbued with a feeling of nostalgia. Russian architects and painters decorated interiors in such styles as neo-Gothic, Pompeian, Rococo, Renaissance, Oriental, and Russian-Byzantine. They also devised and developed methods of ornamenting objects in ways that helped to illustrate the style. The Imperial Glassworks played the leading role in creating works in historical styles, gaining the assistance of St. Petersburg's well-known architects.

Private glassworks used simpler means of making products in the Gothic style, employing colorless glass with an overlay of dark cherry (copper) ruby (no. 42). A certain similarity to Gothic forms can also be seen in the sculptural shape of a decanter of green uranium glass made at the Gus Crystal Works (no. 43).

Characteristics of Oriental art appeared in Russian glass in the early 1830s, and they continued to attract the attention of Russian artists almost until the end of the century.

The art of Egypt, Iran, Turkey, China, and Japan provided a fresh impetus to creativity. The government's desire to influence diplomatic, trade, and cultural relations with Eastern countries was reflected in Russian art. Iran, for example, had always been an attractive market for Russian goods. In the second half of the 19th century, the Russian glass industry tried to compete with the influence of Bohemian glass in the East. Glass hookahs and perfume bottles were also made for Transcaucasia. The Maltsov, Bakhmetiev, and other private glassworks studied the demand for glass objects in the Eastern market and produced especially popular goods in an Eastern style.

The Imperial Glassworks took almost no part in this struggle for the Eastern market. Its contribution to the competition was of a somewhat different nature. As has been mentioned, it made diplomatic presents for the rulers of Eastern countries, as well as items in an Eastern style for the interiors of palaces in St. Petersburg and Moscow. One of this factory's products is a glass vase decorated with 12th-century Iranian motifs (no. 45). Made of opal glass, it bears vegetal designs in the shape of trefoils with spiral shoots and treelike compositions. In medieval times, this ornament represented Paradise; in the 1860s, when the vase was made, the motifs were used merely as decorative elements.

A vase of greenish opal glass, featuring a long neck decorated with a small ring (no. 46), was evidently made for the 1870 exhibition in St. Petersburg. It is covered with enamel paintings of thin olive branches and a flower in a pot framed by arches. There is also ornamentation in the shape of pepper pods, pearls, and diamonds. The pearlike shape of the vessel resembles that of 16th-century Iranian ceramics, while the decoration is similar to that found on earthenware plates. This adaptation of the style of medieval Iranian art is characteristic of art in the period of historicism.

Between the late 1870s and the 1890s, the products of the Imperial Glassworks were influenced by Far Eastern art, especially Chinese porcelain and painted lacquer (nos. 47 and 48). This influence is reflected not only in the careful reproduction of ornaments, but also in the shapes of objects and their range of colors.

Provincial glasshouses were also affected by the passion for Eastern styles. Many items in these styles were produced by the Maltsovs' factory in the late 19th century. Of particular interest is a jug decorated in Iranian style. Its silvered surface and decorations make it look like a metal vessel with engraved ornament (no. 49).

From the 1830s to the 1850s, Russian architects began to build a national style in opposition to European styles that had no roots in Russia. Interest in the art of ancient Rus and folk art stemmed both from the realization that architects were among those who made national history and from a romantic world view that considered Russian antiquities in an entirely new light.

The first glass objects in this Russian style were made at the Imperial Glassworks in the 1860s. Among them are a vase and a decanter decorated with elements of traditional folk art, embroidery, cutting, and painting. Made of blue (cobalt) glass, the vase (no. 50) has the shape of an earthenware milk jar. The artist decorated it with small, geometric ornaments in several friezes resembling the patterns of Russian folk embroideries in cross-, chain-, and satin-stitch. The coloring is similar to the traditional combination of threads in Russian folk embroideries.

The decanter of colorless glass decorated with fretted horses' heads (no. 51) is of particular interest. In painting this object, the artist relied on the traditions of wood carving and embroidery. The decanter was made in 1870, apparently from a design by the outstanding Russian architect V. A. Hartmann. He made more than 600 drawings, including the designs for objects of applied art, for an industrial exhibition held in St. Petersburg in 1870. Hartmann was fascinated by Russian embroideries, and he collected them during his travels through the country. Later, he published them in an album with an introduction written by the Russian critic V. V. Stasov.

A large dinner service with the coat of arms of the Princes Golitsyn, an old Russian aristocratic family, also deserves special mention. Only 11 items of this service are known today: vases for desserts, plates, tureens, and dishes of ruby glass decorated in gold in Russian-Byzantine style (no. 52). What attracts attention is the eclectic touch in the design of this "Golitsyn" service. The shape of the items goes back to the crystal objects of the early 1800s, while the main ornament, in the form of repeated rosettes in circles, has analogies in Byzantine art. The heraldic composition shows a Gothic influence, and the color combination recalls ancient Russian art. This service was made at the Imperial Glassworks in the second half of the 19th century, and it is a striking example of the factory's products in the period of historicism.

At the Maltsovs' glassworks, the Russian style was developed by the talented artist E. Boem. Her works are represented by a *bratina* and a service enameled in the spirit of ancient Russian art (nos. 53 and 54).

The art of engraving also reached considerable heights at the Imperial Glassworks and other Russian glasshouses after 1850. One particularly popular method of decorating crystal in this period of historicism was by using the Renaissance style.

A small and elegant vase of colorless and yellow-stained crystal (no. 55) was made in St. Petersburg in the 1880s. Its central frieze shows engraved putti with symbolic attributes. The lightness and grace of the composition, which is evenly distributed over the body, contrast with the engraved flowers and fruits that are closely grouped on the side of the vase. The cold, shimmering appearance of the lower band of crystal and the goldlike surface layer impart a particular charm to this object.

Masters at the Gus Crystal Works devised a different approach for the decoration of glass. A thick-walled goblet with a lid engraved with the leaves of the acanthus (no. 56) clearly shows that Russian glassmakers were familiar with objects of rock crystal made by Renaissance lapidaries. The models used in engraving at this factory are also items made by folk craftsmen, which clearly display the traditional features of peasant art.

The work of the Travkins and the Zubanovs, glassmakers in a long line of masters at the Maltsov glassworks, reflects a love of nature, the use of bright and rich colors, a fertile imagination, and individual taste. In developing new engraving motifs, they used field and marshland plants and flowers, forest landscapes with animals, and original patterns on the frosted windowpanes of peasant huts.

A crystal jug with large engraved flowers (no. 57) was made at the turn of the 19th century by glassmakers at the Maltsov factory in Gus. It may have been made by the master Ivan Travkin. Another master at the same factory, Pyotr Zubanov, learned the craft of polished engraving from his father, the serf master Maxim Zubanov. He was known for his original engraved pattern called a "light plant." The younger Zubanov created crystal objects that were awarded the highest prize at the 1900 world's fair in Paris.

In the late 19th and early 20th centuries, the period of historicism was replaced by a new style that had a pronounced effect on glassmaking. The forms and decoration scientifically worked out by 19th-century architects, who adhered to the historicist style and used the monuments of antiquity as models, gave way to works of a different artistic nature. Evidently, it was no accident that patterns for glass objects were now designed, not by architects, but by sculptors, painters, or "learned graphic artists." The new style, known in France as *l'Art Nouveau*, is characterized by rounded and tangible volumes, asymmetrical silhouettes, and the free layout of a composition—with emphasis on the enlargement of forms, finesse, and flexibility in the outlines of plant motifs.

Products of the Imperial China and Glass Works became particularly expressive of this new style. Like many western European glasshouses, this factory was intrigued by the glass made at Emile Gallé's firm in France. Among the items in this style from the Russian glassworks are an 1899 crystal vase with engraved sea shells (no. 58) and a small ovoid vase with multiple layers of bluish turquoise glass (no. 59). This object, which dates from 1898, is decorated with leaves and a snake in the cameo-carving technique used by Gallé.

Masters at the Imperial Glassworks were also influenced by the traditional treatment of semiprecious stones. Their cutting made it possible to bring out all the color and textural wealth of their material. Vases from the factory were made in the art nouveau style at a time when the artistic department was headed by Ivan Murinov, a practical painter described by his contemporaries as a "man of excellent artistic taste." Murinov combined his work at the glasshouse with teaching at the Baron Stieglitz School of Technical Drawing in St. Petersburg. This school, which enjoyed a high reputation in Russia, trained specialists for the national art industry.

The collection of glass objects from the Gus Crystal Works provides an idea of how the art nouveau style was reproduced in items intended for the mass market. Vases and lamp stands with landscapes or large flowers figured prominentaly in its list of products. They were made in the manner of Gallé with the use of deep etching (no. 60). The factory also employed the decorating methods and techniques of Austrian and Bohemian glassworks, especially those of the firm owned by the widow of Johann Lötz, where iridization was widely used (nos. 61 and 62). No preference was given to any particular technique. On the contrary, the impression is that masters at the Gus glasshouse made use of the entire gamut of artistic methods employed at European glassworks at the turn of the 20th century (nos. 60–70).

In addition to their works of art, private glasshouses produced large numbers of "popular" products. They developed numerous forms of household glass with standardized decoration. The glassmaking skills of the workers permitted the production of many dinner services. Three such services, intended for a broad range of consumers, are featured here. Two of them are made of colorless non-lead glass, while the third is of lead crystal. The glass in one set has a little engraving (no. 68). Another service was decorated with mechanically wound threading (no. 69).

Crystal objects were prominently featured on the product list of the Gus glassworks. They were usually decorated with traditional cut patterns (no. 70). Many crystal items made at the Gus factory were intended to have metal mounts. Cheaper items of simple glass were set in white metal, while objects with rich diamond facets were framed with silver.

Silver settings for crystal products were manufactured by many jewelry companies in Russia. The world-famous firm of Carl Fabergé was also involved in making these items. The owner, using the latest technological achievements and the best traditions of the European jeweler's art, attained great popularity both inside and outside Russia. His firm used the services of the country's best artists, architects, painters, and sculptors, as well as many talented jewelers.

One of Fabergé's decanters displays an original cut pattern known as "Russian Stone." Created at the Imperial Glassworks in the 1820s, it was widely used at other Russian glasshouses (no. 71)—and even in the United States, where it is known as the "Russian" pattern. Another decanter is decorated with deep cutting in the art nouveau style, which is balanced by a strict and simple setting (no. 72).

Russian glassmaking at the turn of the 20th century featured an extremely wide range of stylistic trends, each of them relying on a vast arsenal of technical means (no. 73). Perhaps the most characteristic feature of Russian glassmaking was the fact that all of its artists were located at the glassworks. Russian glassmakers did not know the studio system. Professional artists were a rarity, and their employment was the privilege of the Imperial Glassworks. The quality of the great majority of glass products made in Russian factories was determined by the skills of their workmen.

Soviet Glass

Liudmila Kazakova

THE HISTORY OF SOVIET GLASSMAKING can be divided into two periods. The first period began with the 1917 Socialist Revolution and ended in the early 1950s. The artistic development of Soviet glassmaking started in the difficult post-revolutionary years. Because of an economic blockade and an acute fuel shortage, only the main glassworks were in operation: the Gus and Dyat'kovo Crystal Works (the former Maltsov factory), the Nikol'skoye-Bakhmetiev glasshouse (the Krasnyy Gigant Works since the 1930s), and the Chudovo glassworks. All of them mass-produced the most essential glassware: lamps, jars, bottles, and drinking glasses.

Of the works made in the 1920s, only a few examples are known that reflect the new times and the new way of life. Soviet emblems, the hammer and sickle, and the subject of construction (seen on the vase *Five-Year-Plan in Four Years*, no. 74) were employed for the first time. In the 1930s, the main effort was aimed at the technical overhaul of the glasshouses, increasing their rate of output, and expanding their range of products. The largest glassworks again began to produce crystal items.

The mass-produced articles were based on the existing patterns of the glassworks because of the limited number of artists there. One of the first glass artists was A. Ya. Jakobson, who had come to the Nikol'skoye-Bakhmetiev factory before the revolution. Most of the designers of patterns were self-taught masters who came from long lines of glassmakers; they had been well trained by their fathers and grandfathers. Others were practical artists without specialized education.

The development of glassmaking was hampered by a mistaken perception of the artist's role in industry. Many theoreticians believed that the mass production of forms and patterns made the problem of their artistic quality irrelevant. In the late 1930s, when artists did begin to work in the production sphere, they never created or designed industrial models. Their role was limited to decorating the existing forms of glassware (nos. 74–78).

The late 1930s—a time linked with the activities of the Leningrad group of artists—was a truly innovative period in the history of Soviet glass. In 1940, the well-known sculptor V. I. Mukhina and a group of scientific and cultural experts (including the professor N. N. Kachalov and the writer A. N. Tolstoy) devised a plan to revive the art of glassmaking. This plan involved setting up an experimental workshop for making prototypes of glassware at the Leningrad mirror factory. Mukhina, A. A. Uspensky, and A. N. Tyrsa were artists who asserted new esthetic principles based on a new understanding of the "truthfulness" of the material and constructive thinking in creating forms. Within a very short time (1940–1941), dozens of works that became classics of Soviet glass were created.

The fact that such an outstanding sculptor as Vera Mukhina turned to glass was of fundamental importance. The sculptural use of the material led to a new method of producing subject forms—seen in such vases as *Aster* (no. 79), *Lotus*, and *Turnip*—and of creating glass sculptures—including *Torso* (no. 80), *A Sitting Girl*, and *Grief*. The development of models for mass production was combined with the making of individual works of art. Mukhina understood and affirmed the major esthetic role of decorative and applied art as an index of the people's culture.

Vases, beakers, jugs, and goblets made by A. Uspensky in 1940 and 1941 are marked by a particular elegance of outline and a correlation of proportions that impart simplicity and monumentality (no. 81). The purely utilitarian forms reveal the remarkable power of spirit and beauty expressed by blowing simple, smooth glass, both colorless and colored. In his work, Uspensky always proceeded from the nature of the material. Sometimes, colored stripes were added to transparent, drop-like forms to underline the constructive basis of the glass. Uspensky was undoubtedly one of the leading artists in the world of glassmaking at that time. These artists revealed the poetry and beauty of smooth, transparent glass in everyday, practical forms.

The utilitarian objects made by N. Tyrsa reflect the same natural beauty of the material and a similar concern for proportions and silhouettes. Despite the extremely short period of Uspensky's and Tyrsa's creative activity (less than two years), these artists were unusually productive. They also played important roles in the history of Soviet glassmaking, and their works are among the classics of this art.

In the late 1930s, technical advances in the melting, working, and decoration of glass made it possible to start using it extensively in large-scale art. The construction of the first stations of the Moscow subway and the pavilions of the All-Union Agricultural Exhibition, as well as the USSR's participation in two world's fairs—Paris (1937) and New York (1939), contributed to the appearance of monumental works of glass: stained glass windows, mosaics, lamps, and fountains. For example, a crystal fountain made for the New York world's fair by the sculptor I. M. Chaikov and the engineer F. S. Entelis was a unique work from both artistic and technical points of view. This fountain, 4.2 meters high, became a classic of its time. Its basin was made of a thick, solid sheet of crystal, and nearly all the methods of glass decoration known in those days were used in ornamenting the complex structure.

Stars of ruby glass were made for the spires of the Moscow Kremlin's towers to mark the 20th anniversary of the 1917 revolution. The first Soviet stained glass windows appeared between 1936 and 1939. Also among the high artistic achievements were the mosaics for the Mayakovskaya Station of the Moscow subway, designed by A. A. Deineka. The first successful uses of glass in architecture attracted a good deal of attention and showed the important role that it could have in combining art and architecture.

The creative quest for ways of renewing the artistic language of glassmaking was interrupted by the outbreak of World War II. During the war, glassworks concentrated on the manufacture of vital products for the country, and the output of decorative objects was drastically reduced. Restoration and overhaul of the glasshouses began in the first postwar years. The initial priority was arranging for the production of simple tableware, but the problems of artistic development was also tackled gradually. Many professional artists who had graduated from glassmaking programs at art schools in Moscow, Leningrad, and Tallinn came to work in the industry. This development paved the way for a new phase in the history of Soviet glassmaking. Among the artists who found employment in the research laboratories of the country's glassworks were E. Krimmer, B. Smirnov (nos. 84 and 90), N. Eismont, and Ye. Yanovskaya in Leningrad, and G. Yegorov, A. Lipsksaya, Ye. Rogov (no. 95), N. Rostovtseva, N. Tarkovskaya, and Ye. Shuvalov in Gus' Khrustal'nyy and Dyat'kovo. Those who began their glassmaking careers in the mid-1950s were A. Maveva, H. Põld (no. 85), S. Raudvee, V. Murakhver, L. Myagkova, L. Smirnova, L. Jurgen, and the Moscow artists G. Antonova (no. 101), S. Beskinskaya, O. Kobylinskaya, I. Nevskaya, S. Ryazanova, A. Stepanova, and A. Silko.

Existing factory patterns were dominant in the output of mass-produced glassware during the early postwar period. The new constellation of artists began their search for stylistic innovation at a time when basic artistic attitudes were being shaped in decorative and applied art. It was a complex and contradictory process. In the 1950s, the prevailing tendency in glass was toward the formal decoration of objects without considering their function. At times, fine arts principles were mechanically extended to the creation of objects. However, in the best items made during those years, artists carried on the work started by V. Mukhina.

One of the characteristic trends in the art of the 1950s was a return to the traditions of folk glassmaking, which included focusing on the forms and techniques of blown glass. All sorts of figure-shaped vessels (e.g., decanters in the shape of roosters and women) were created, and these objects were decorated with bright, molded ornaments. Modern ideas about glass forms were also seen in the collection of objects prepared for Expo '58, the world's fair in Brussels. Many of the Soviet displays received the highest awards at that exhibition.

The late 1950s and early 1960s opened the second period in the development of Soviet glassmaking. In the 1960s, the stylistic peculiarities of decorative and applied art, as well as the demand for a strict, rational simplicity of form, were also reflected in glass. The main distinguishing feature of the creative effort was a fundamentally different approach to designing the form of an object. This approach was accompanied by a reduction in—and sometimes a rejection of—decoration, as was reflected in the corresponding notions of a "pure" form in glass and a "white" line in china. The idea of pure form (Uspensky's glass was one model) was a kind of reaction against the ornamental extravagances of the preceding period. Works of various artists seemed to embody the requirements of standard industrial models. The All-Union Exhibition in Moscow, "Art in Everyday Life," proclaimed a new esthetic program for renovating the object medium. Designers displaying art in keeping with this program included A. Astvatsaturyan (no. 87), A. Ostroumov (no. 99), V. Filatov (no. 83), V. Korneyev (no. 89), V. Shevchenko (no. 88), M. Grabar, V. Murakhver, and L. Myagkova. Artists created dozens of models for mass production, items issued by glassworks were considerably revised, and an attempt was made at the Neman and Gus' Khrustal'nyy factories to amend the means of expression on pressed glass.

Several collections of household sulphide glass were made at the Krasnyy Mai glasshouse and the Dyat'kovo Crystal Works. Sulphide glass, which was developed by A. Kirjenen and E. Ivanova, fills a special page in the history of Soviet glassmaking. Having emerged from the Leningrad laboratory in the early 1950s, it became a material that provided a new esthetic value. Such artists as S. Beskinskaya, V. Shevchenko (no. 88), L. Kuchinskaya, and V. Khrolov devoted their work to mastering the new material. Beskinskaya's glass is marked by poetical metaphor and a concern for color, Shevchenko's compositions (no. 88) assert the sculptural principles of form building, and Kuchinskaya's works reflect the influence of colored plastic images. Khrolov carried on the folklore line, while works by A. Novikova and S. Konoplyova show their attention to painting and technique. T. Sazhin (no. 120) and L. Fomina used sulphide glass in large-scale forms.

By the mid-1960s, there were departments of design at nearly all of the glassworks in the Soviet Union. These laboratories employed new graduates from the Mukhina Higher School of Industrial Design in Leningrad and the Moscow Higher School of Industrial Design. V. Muratov (nos. 98 and 118), F. Ibragimov (no. 96), O. Kozlova (no. 116), A. Kurilov (no. 108), S. Verin, and R. Aksenov worked in Gus' Khrustal'nyy; V. Shevchenko (no. 88) and M. Grabar came to Dyat'kovo; and V. Khrolov, L. Kuchinskaya, and A. Novikova started at the Krasnyy Mai glasshouse. Most of the factory artists combined the development of models for mass production with the creation of unique items for display at exhibitions. Other artists worked on contracts signed with unions or government institutions.

The traditions and production requirements of the glassworks undoubtedly determine their artistic styles. For example, designers at the Gus factory are developing the art of engraving, carved plant ornaments, blown objects in the form of animals, and colored crystal. Their counterparts at the Leningrad glasshouse are following the traditions of classical strictness and simplicity in the faceted patterns of crystal surfaces, providing for the structural forms of their items. The Dyat'kovo Crystal Works is refining its technique of enameling on simple clear and colored glass. At the same time, glassware made to individual designs is revealing innovations such as relief decoration in crystal in the works made by V. Muratov (nos. 98 and 118), A. Ostroumov (no. 99), L. Jurgen, I. Machnev (no. 107), and B. Fyodorov, and a colored sculptural line in sulphide glass (V. Shevchenko, no. 88). Despite all their differences in creative style, works made to these designs reflect the continuing search for imagery and associative expression in glass while preserving all the natural qualities of the material—its glitter, purity, transparency, color, and texture.

In the late 1960s and 1970s, glassmaking went beyond the framework of object forms to enter the province of sculpture. This gradual and important change was the result of the designers' experiments with forms. The growing understanding of the sculptural value of glass developed by enlarging dish forms, by abandoning a utilitarian approach, and by realizing the independent spiritual value of a glass object. Assisting this process was the expanding role of the decorative arts in the cultural advancement of society. Decorative artists faced the tasks of esthetically organizing their glass and synthesizing their art with other arts, especially architecture. The mastering of architectural space prompted glassmakers to consider new forms of decorative glass. A series of colored sculptural compositions and ensembles resulted, along with a period of individual experiments and styles. Other factors contributing to this process were a rapid increase in exhibitions (participation both at home and abroad) and an influx of young artists that raised the level of experimentation. These designers included V. Kasatkin (no. 117), I. Machnev (no. 107), B. Fyodorov (no. 105), V. Kotov (no. 110), A. and G. Ivanov (no. 113), A. Bokotei, L. Savelyeva (nos. 109 and 119), N. Uryadova (no. 112), N. Tikhomirova (no. 103), and N. Goncharova (no. 106).

Unlike the 1960s, which were marked by a search for stylistic unity, the trend in the 1970s and especially the 1980s is toward varied materials and individual expression and techniques. It was no coincidence that numerous individual and group exhibitions, demonstrating a broad range of creative personalities, were presented during this time.

When discussing masters of Soviet glassmaking, we must first mention B. Smirnov, whose always unpredictable art has also served as a signpost. Smirnov set demanding goals for himself, and he met these challenges with remarkable imagination. *A Festive Table* (1967) is one of his most important works. In this ensemble of more than 120 items, conceived as representing a popular festival, the artist proceeded from traditional methods, which were widely known in old Russian glassmaking. Smirnov created his composition *Man, Horse, Dog, and Bird* (no. 90) as a modern sculpture of colored glass.

The development of glassblowing traditions in contemporary glass scuplture, a typical feature of Soviet glassmaking, was stimulated to some degree by Smirnov's works, although each artist showed his own attitude toward this subject. The technique of glassblowing resulted in an interesting series of developments in the use of color and sculptural elements in sulphide glass.

S. Beskinskaya was one of the first artists to discover the beauty of sulphide glass. Together with the technician E. Ivanova, she created purely utilitarian objects that are now considered classics (the services "Brown Cow" and "Kitchen"). Her later ensembles combine the decorative properties of glass with its unlimited possibilities of form and color.

Works by V. Shevchenko (no. 88) reveal an entirely different process of creative thinking. His sulphide glass objects considerably enriched our ideas of the sculptural possibilities of this material. His composition *Metamorphoses*, which features apertures in its form, reveals the dynamic life of glass in relation to space. Shevchenko's decorative ensembles contain a hidden inner force, a sense of tension (the forms seem to be penetrating one another). The impression is heightened by the textural contrast of light and shade of the surface and the emotional charge of color. This designer was also responsible for some interesting technical discoveries that enhanced his art.

The works of D. and L. Shushkanov (nos. 91 and 111) occupy a special place in the search for the sculptural value of colored glass. The virtuoso painting technique that distinguishes each of their creations constitutes an artistic phenomenon. Various tints in the thick mass of glass are seen as complex painted structures of color, light, and air. The tornado-like, pulsating mass inside the glass objects is moderated by the strong, calm forms of the objects with smoothly flashed edges.

The spatial sculptural quest in decorative art during the second half of the 1970s and 1980s affected various genres—tapestry, ceramics, metal, and jewelry. This creative task gave rise to numerous new ideas and led to the discovery of various technical methods. The sensation of space was expressed in a particularly graphic form in glass because of its transparency and its ability to absorb and reflect light. The subject of space captured the artists' imagination because it offered the possibility of solving the problem of man and the medium, of man and nature. As a result, a new type of glass object came into being.

The broadly interpreted notion of space was presented in terms of a world view in Smirnov's *Weightlessness* and *Solaris*. The cosmic sense of space is peculiar to the glass objects made by L. Savelyeva. The strong, hollow forms full of light and air are animated by the presence of images of people and landscapes. The artist's method provides an organic blend of glass space and painting. Man is pictured in a state of contemplation as part of the natural environment in *Self-Portrait in Space* (no. 109). The enameling manages to achieve a remarkably wide range of expression in conveying human feelings. Man is made commensurate with space through motion in it. The flat silhouette of a figure, foreshortened differently on each of the two sides of the form, is included in the inner mass.

Optical glass objects present a different concept of spatial relationships. The use of geometric form, which is not very common in Soviet glassmaking, has recently been developed in a rather interesting manner in the works of the young artists O. Podobedova, M. Lisitsina, and N. Uryadova (no. 112). The main artistic sense of these ground objects, made from glass of extremely high purity and transparency, is their interaction with the space around them by means of light. The blocks of glass focus and reflect the object world. At the same time, optical effects create a micro-world of their own.

The intellectual comprehension of form, characteristic of creative arts in the late 1980s, has led to revising the methods and techniques in every area of glassmaking. The broadening of creative problems and the deepening of the image structure in works of art dictate a different approach. For example, the decorative principles of working with crystal, which seemed unshakable, were supplanted by a sculptural approach to the problem of form. Light and sculptural modeling has brought about innovations in the creation of form. The visual effect of the works by V. Muratov (nos. 98 and 118), B. Fyodorov (no. 105), A. Ostroumov (no. 99), and I. Machnev (no. 107) is achieved by contrasting frosted and semi-transparent textures resembling marble, the light and shade modeling of the smooth outlines of silhouettes, and the mysterious glimmer in the thick of the material. Significantly, the sandblasting technique is becoming a favorite method, making it possible to emphasize the sculptural quality of the form.

In the realm of engraved glass, where purely graphic methods are used by such artists as H. Põld (no. 85), there is also interest in combining sculptural relief with effective optical methods. The latter trend can be observed in works by A. Ivanov (no. 113) and A. Kurilov (no. 108). In abstract glass sculpture, image-bearing expressiveness emerges from the very nature of the material—its plasticity, color, light refraction, and structural decoration. This is shown in works by V. Pogrebnoy (no. 104), V. Muratov (no. 98 and 118), and V. Kasatkin (no. 117).

The sculptural approach explains the appearance and development of the glass still life. Such works were created first in non-lead glass (e.g., by G. Antonova, no. 101) and then in crystal, depicting flowers, fruits, and other objects. The motif of the molded flower has a long tradition in Russian glassmaking; in the 19th century, craftsmen liked to make bunches of glass flowers. These skills survive at the Gus' Khrustal'nyy, Dyat'kovo, and Krasnyy Mai glassworks. Artists have given this motif a new life by incorporating it into their search for new decorative forms. It is interesting to note that the molded flower motif gave rise to numerous solutions in such monumental glass forms as stained glass windows, lamps, and fountains. The subject of glass flowers also became part of G. Antonova's, A. Stepanova's, and I. Marshumova's (nos. 92 and 93) creative activity. Decorative compositions by Marshumova and L. Urtayeva and object compositions by I. Machnev (no. 107) are examples of glass still lifes.

Glass painting is represented by the works of J. Manelis (no. 102) and V. Kotov (no. 110), who demonstrate fundamentally different approaches in their creative tasks. Manelis, using luster colors with an iridescent effect, conveys sensations of light and air in landscape motifs. The glass surface appears to enter a picturesque, colorful fabric, imparting lightness and transparency to it. Kotov's work devoted to the well-known primitivist painter N. Pirosmani is made in a manner that corresponds to the latter's paintings. Glass that is almost black, like Pirosmani's canvases, is decorated with motifs that were much admired by the painter. The work is, in fact, a paraphrase of his favorite subjects.

The development of Soviet glass today is linked with worldwide progress in glassmaking. The growing number of international activities—exhibitions, symposiums, and exchanges of information—give a fresh impetus to individual experiments and creative competition. The studio movement, in which artists are both designers and makers of their works, is raising glass to a new esthetic level—a level that signifies its expanding influence in world culture. Soviet glass is playing an important role in this process.

ILLUSTRATIONS

1. *Kumgan* (Ewer)
Izmailovo glassworks, near Moscow,
late 17th century.

2. Beaker
Engraved Russian double-headed eagle and
inscription: Vivat Czar Peter Alekseevich.
Yamburg glassworks, 1710–1720.

3. Covered Goblet
Engraved portrait of Empress Anna Ivanovna.
Yamburg glassworks, 1730–1740.

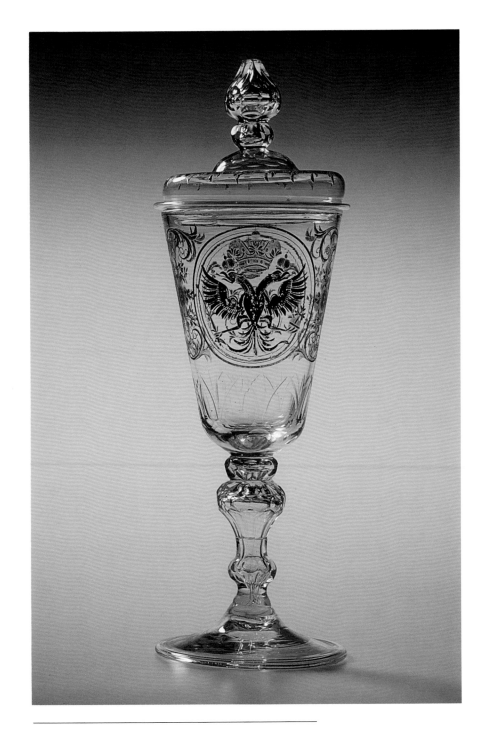

4. Covered Goblet
Engraved monogram of Empress Elizabeth Petrovna
and Russian eagle.
St. Petersburg Glassworks, mid-18th century.

5. Beaker
Engraved portrait of
Empress Elizabeth Petrovna.
St. Petersburg Glassworks,
1750–1760.

6. Covered Goblet
Engraved portrait of
Empress Elizabeth Petrovna.
St. Petersburg Glassworks,
1750–1760.

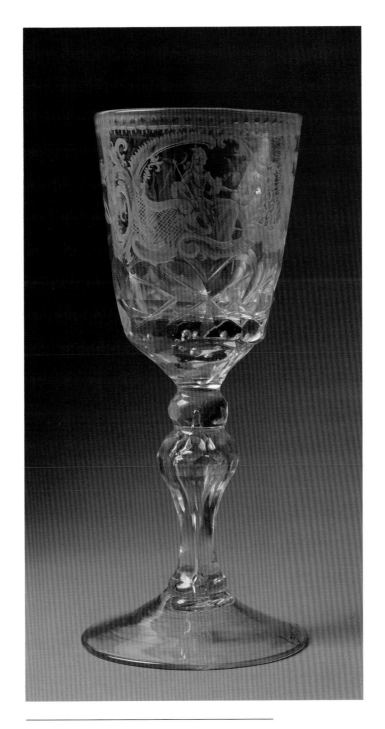

7. Goblet
Engraved portrait of Empress Catherine II.
Made at Naziya, engraved in St. Petersburg,
1770–1780.

8. Covered Goblet
Engraved allegorical composition of
Empress Catherine II.
Made at Naziya, engraved St. Petersburg,
1770–1780.

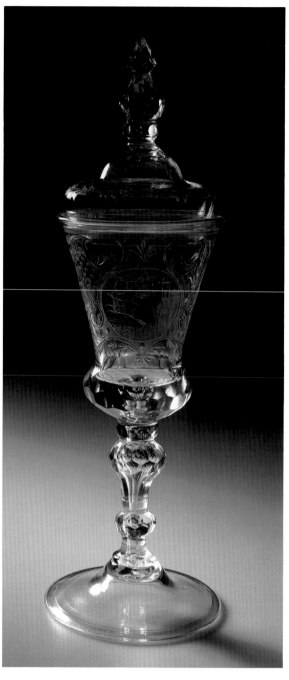

9. Covered Goblet
Engraved with reindeer.
Vasily Maltsov's glassworks,
engraved by Stepan Lagutin,
mid-18th century.

10. Figural Bear-Bottle
Unknown Russian glassworks,
first half of the 18th century.

11. Bottle
Enameled lion and inscription: "Lion."
Unknown Russian glassworks,
first half of the 18th century.

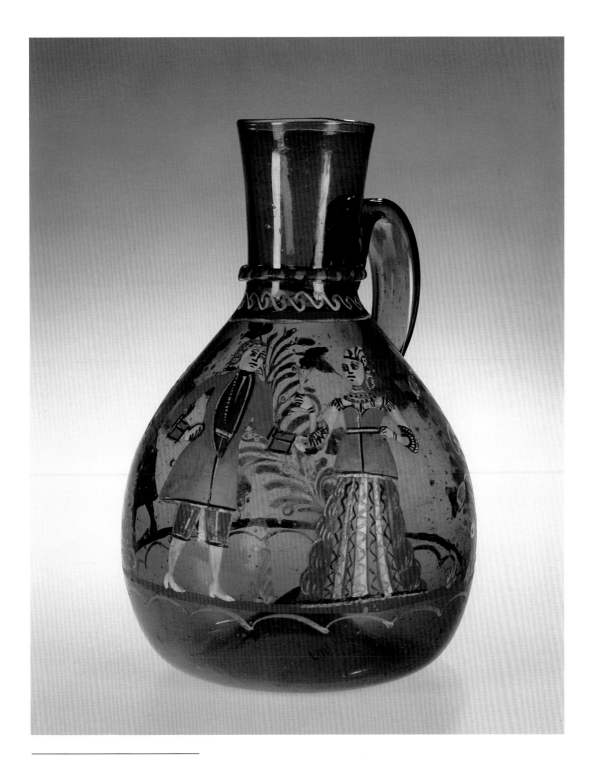

12. Jug
Enameled holiday scene.
Unknown Russian glassworks,
second half of the 18th century.

13. Mosaic Portrait of Pyotr Ivanovich Shuvalov
Workshop of Mikhail Lomonosov, 1758.

14. Icon, *Our Lady of Cyprus*
Russia, late 18th century.

15. Covered Mug
Imperial Glassworks, late 18th century.

16. Decanter with Stopper
Imperial Glassworks,
late 18th or early 19th century.

17. Covered Goblet
Imperial Glassworks,
late 18th or early 19th century.

18. Mug with Landscape
Imperial Glassworks,
end of the 18th century.

19. Easter Egg with Landscape
Imperial Glassworks,
end of the 18th century.

20. Discus with Star
Imperial Glassworks, early 19th century.

21. Covered Beaker
Bakhmetiev's glassworks,
late 18th or early 19th century.

22. Wineglass
Gilded monogram of
Alexander Pavlovich,
later Emperor Alexander I.
Alexander Vershinin (?),
Bakhmetiev's glassworks, 1795.

23. *Shtof* (Vodka Bottle)
Enameled Russian double-headed eagle.
F. G. Orlov's glassworks, about 1796–1801.

24. Cup and Saucer
F. G. Orlov's glassworks, late 18th century.

**25. Decanter with
Four Compartments**
Imperial Glassworks, late 18th
or early 19th century.

26. Pieces from the "Orlov" Service
Imperial Glassworks, late 18th or early 19th century.

---

27. Double-Walled Tumbler
Rural landscape with people in boat.
Bakhmetiev's glassworks, early 1800s.

28. Tripod Vase
Andrei Voronikhin, Imperial Glassworks,
early 1800s.

29. Tripod Vase
Ivan Ivanov, Imperial Glassworks,
1820–1830.

30. Covered Goblet with Victory
Imperial Glassworks, after 1814.

31. Covered Mug
Portrait of Count Wittgenstein.
Imperial Glassworks, 1820–1830.

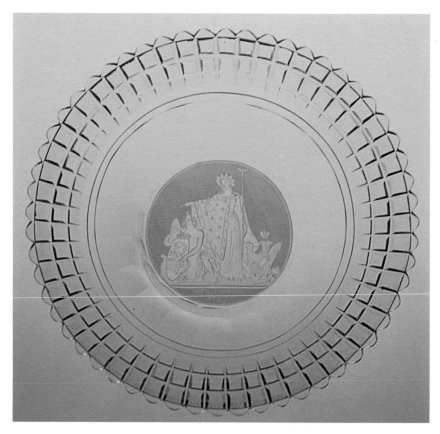

32. Plate, *Peace to Europe*
Imperial Glassworks,
1830–1840.
Engraved by J. Gube,
after the original by F. Tolstoy.

33. Medallion, *The Battle of Borodino*
Imperial Glassworks, from medallion by F. Tolstoy,
1830–1840.

34. Vase
Imperial Glassworks, 1830–1840.

35. Footed Bowl
Imperial Glassworks,
first third of the 19th century.

36. Footed Bowl
Imperial Glassworks, 1830–1840.

37. Decanter with Stopper
Imperial Glassworks,
second quarter of the 19th century.

38. Decanter with Stopper
Imperial Glassworks,
second half of the 19th century.

39. Goblet
Coat of arms of the Kolokoltsov family.
Dyat'kovo Crystal Works, 1860–1870.

41. Pieces of the "Gothic" Service
Ivan Ivanov (?), Imperial Glassworks,
second quarter of the 19th century.

42. Covered Mug
Maltsov's glassworks,
second quarter of the 19th century.

40. Chalice
Unknown Russian glassworks,
second quarter of the 19th century.

44. Perfume Bottle
Imperial Glassworks,
second quarter of the 19th century.

43. Decanter with Stopper
Gus Crystal Works, mid-19th century.

45. Vase
Decorated with Iranian motifs.
Imperial Glassworks,
second half of the 19th century.

46. Vase
Imperial Glassworks,
1870–1880.

47. Vase
Imperial Glassworks,
second half of the 19th century.

48. Vase
Imperial Glassworks, 1880–1890.

49. Jug
Gus Crystal Works, about 1893.

50. Covered Vase
Victor Hartmann (?),
Imperial Glassworks, 1870–1880.

52. Covered Bowl and Plate
from a Service of the Princes Golitsyn
Imperial Glassworks, 1860–1880.

51. Decanter with Stopper
Victor Hartmann (?),
Imperial Glassworks, 1870–1880.

53. *Bratina*
Yelizaveta Boem,
Dyat'kovo Crystal Works,
1875–1885.

54. Part of a Service for Vodka
Yelizaveta Boem, Dyat'kovo Crystal Works, 1897.

55. Vase
Imperial Glassworks, 1880–1890.

56. Covered Goblet
Gus Crystal Works, end of the 19th century.

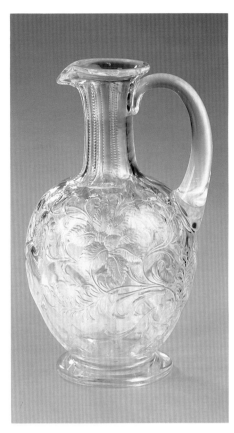

57. Jug
Possibly engraved by Ivan Travkin.
Gus Crystal Works, early 20th century.

58. Vase
Imperial China and
Glass Works, 1899.

59. Vase
Imperial China and Glass Works, 1898.

60. Vase
Gus Crystal Works, early 20th century.

62. Bowl
Gus Crystal Works, early 20th century.

61. Vase
Gus Crystal Works, early 20th century.

63. Vase
Gus Crystal Works, early 20th century.

64. Vase
Gus Crystal Works,
early 20th century.

65. Compote for Jam
Gus Crystal Works, early 20th century.

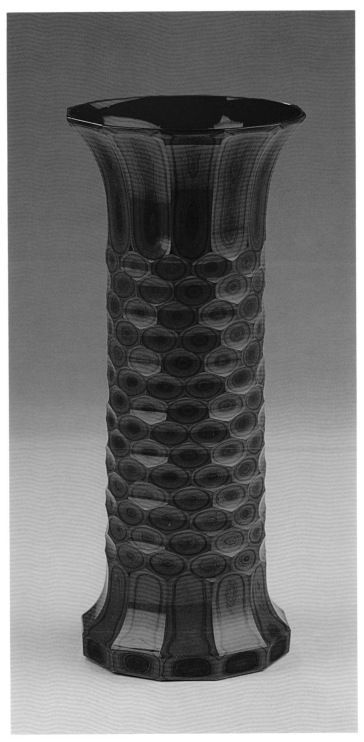

66. Vase
Gus Crystal Works,
early 20th century.

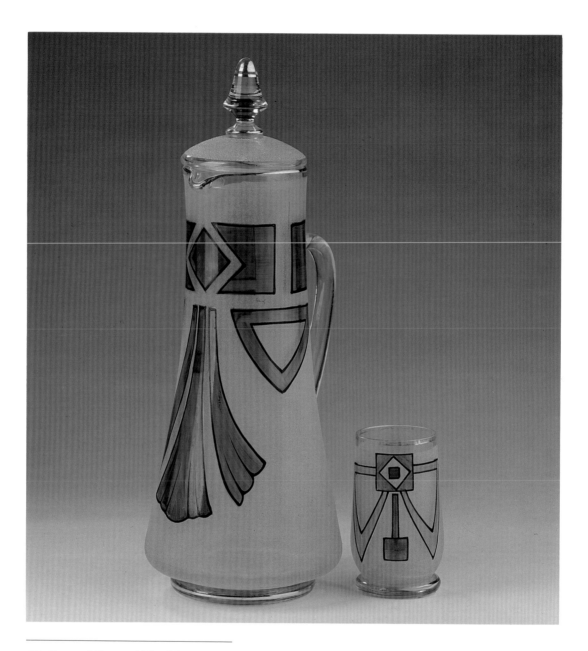

67. Covered Jug and Tumbler
Gus Crystal Works, early 20th century.

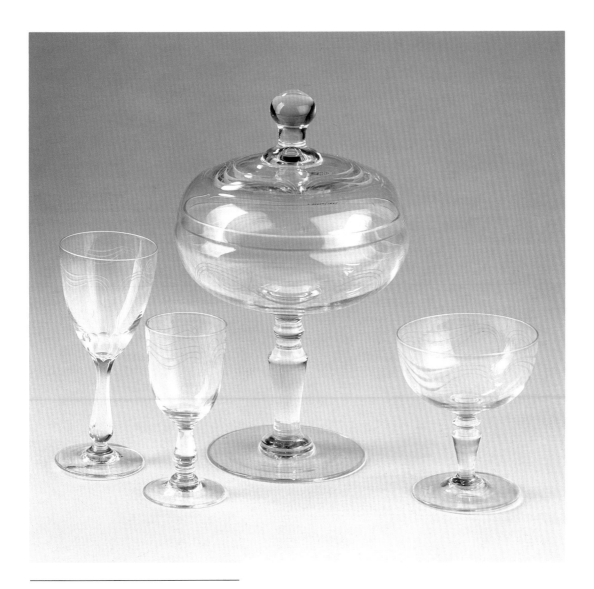

68. Pieces of a Table Service
Gus Crystal Works, early 20th century.

69. Pieces of a Table Service
Gus Crystal Works, early 20th century.

70. Pieces of a Table Service
Gus Crystal Works, early 20th century.

71. Decanter
Unknown glassworks and C. Fabergé firm,
Moscow, early 20th century.

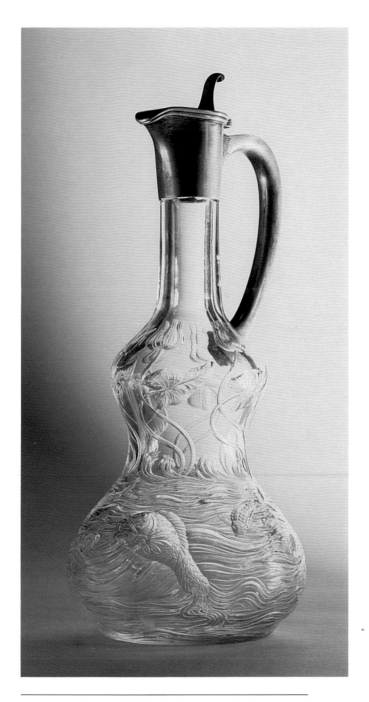

72. Jug
Imperial China and Glass Works and C. Fabergé firm,
late 19th or early 20th century.

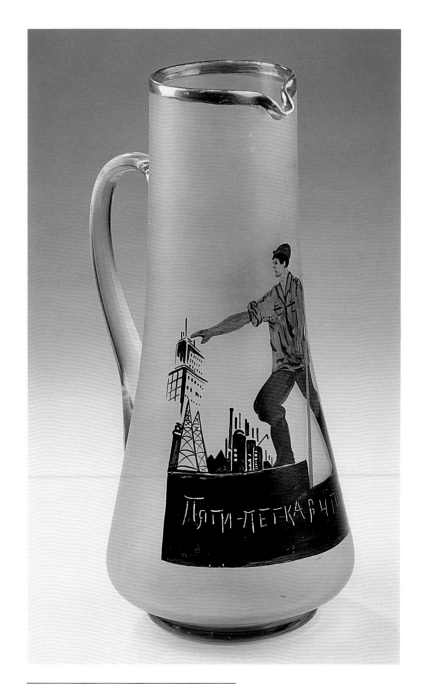

74. Jug, *Five-Year Plan in Four Years*
Gus Crystal Works, about 1929–1932.

73. Vase
Imperial China and Glass Works, 1897.

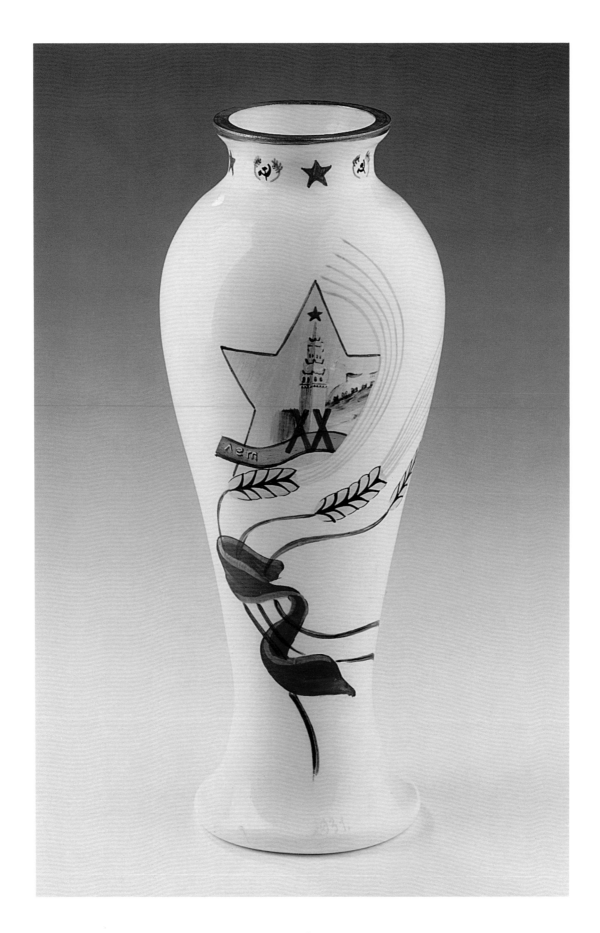

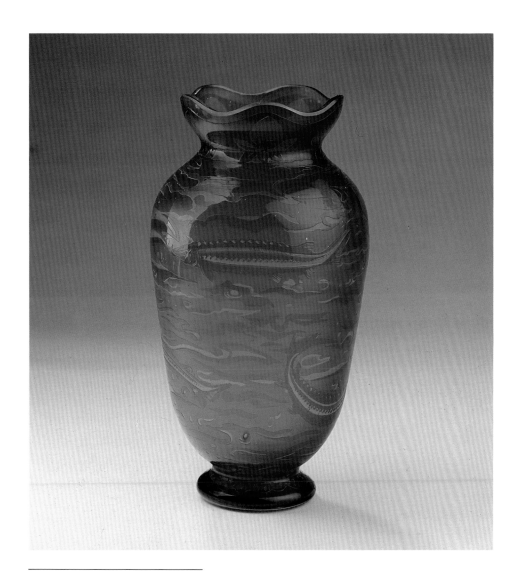

76. Vase, *Sea Depths*
Gus Crystal Works, about 1939.

75. Vase with Soviet Emblems
Gus Crystal Works, 1937.

77. Vase
Gus Crystal Works, about 1947.

78. Wash Bowl and Pitcher
Gus Crystal Works, late 1940s.

79. Vase, *Aster*
Vera Mukhina, 1940–1941.

80. *Torso*
Vera Mukhina, 1940–1941,
cast in 1949.

81. Vase
Alexei Uspensky, 1940.

82. Vase
Gus Crystal Works, 1950–1960.

83. Vase, *Outer Space*
Vladimir Filatov, 1959.

84. Vase, *Glassblowers*
Boris Smirnov, 1961.

85. Vase, *Electrification*
Helle Põld, 1968.

86. *Troika*
Yuri Byakov, 1968.

87. Vase, *Neptune*
Aknuny Astvatsaturyan, 1968.

88. Vase, *Nests*
Victor Shevchenko, 1968.

89. *Foma and Yeryoma*
Vladimir Korneyev, 1967.

90. *Man, Horse, Dog, Bird*
Boris Smirnov, 1970.

91. Vase, *Mars*
Dmitry Shushkanov and
Ludmila Shushkanova, 1973.

92. *Bee*
Irina Marshumova, 1974.

93. *Dragonfly*
Irina Marshumova, 1974.

94. *Venice*
Vladimir Zhokhov, 1974.

95. Vase, *Forest Ranges*
Yevgheny Rogov, 1971.

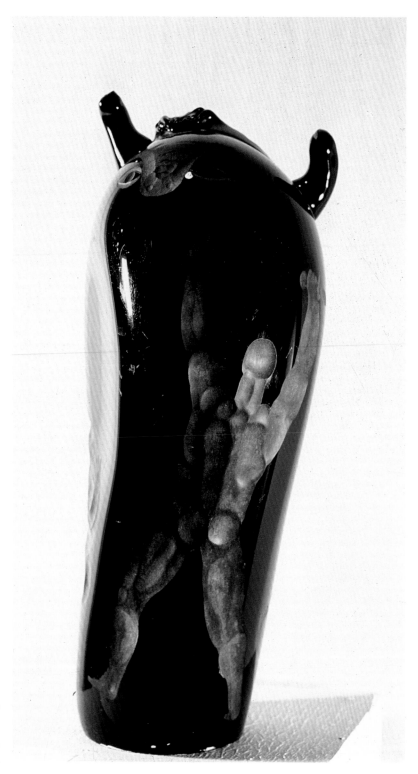

96. *Minotaur*
Fidail Ibragimov, 1968.

97. *He and She*
Yekaterina Yanovskaya, 1970.

98. *The Arctic*
Vladimir Muratov, 1974.

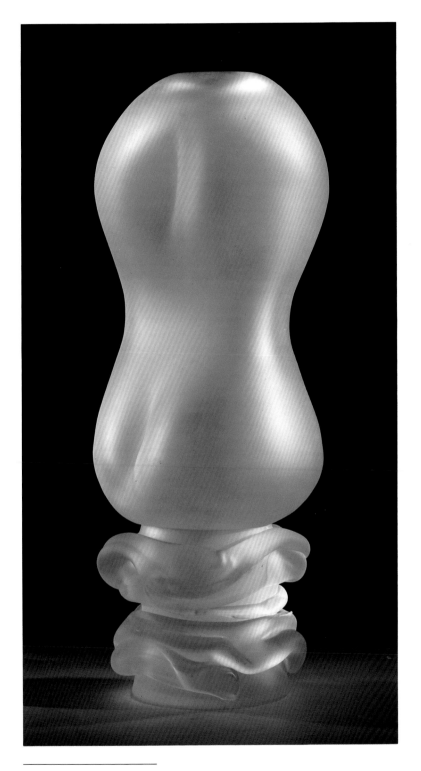

99. *Galatea*
Adolf Ostroumov, 1974.

100. Vase, *Autumn*
Leida Jurgen, 1974.

101. *Summer*
Galina Antonova, 1975.

102. *Mountebanks*
Yuri Manelis, 1978.

103. *Chuckotka*
Natal'ya Tikhomirova, 1975.

104. *A Wind of Wandering*
Vladimir Pogrebnoy, 1978.

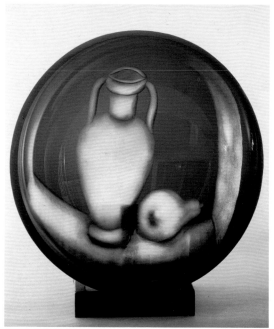

105. *Dream*
Boris Fyodorov, 1981.

106. *Summer Garden*
Natal'ya Goncharova, 1981.

107. *Listening to Stravinsky*
Ivan Machnev, 1981.

108. Bowl, *Inspiration*
Adolf Kurilov, 1982.

109. *Self-Portrait in Space*
Lyubov Savelyeva, 1982.

110. Dedicated to *Pirosmani*
Vladimir Kotov, 1984.

111. *India*
Dmitry Shushkanov and
Ludmila Shushkanova, 1984.

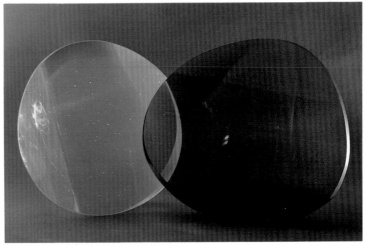

112. *And the Sky Is Full of Stars*
Natal'ya Uryadova, 1985.

113. *White Nights*
Alexander Ivanov, 1986.

114. *My Muse*
Svetlana Ryazanova, 1984.

115. Vases from *The South*
Vyacheslav Zaitzev, 1985.

116. Vases, *Pairs*
Olga Kozlova, 1987.

117. *Emotion*
Vladimir Kasatkin, 1987.

118. *The Epoch*
Vladimir Muratov, 1987.

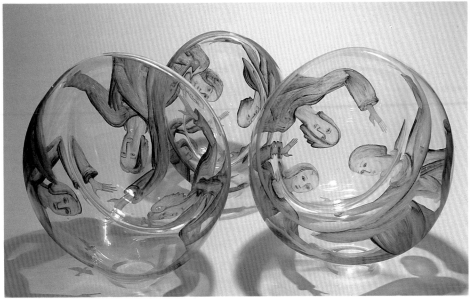

119. *The Space-3*
Lyubov Savelyeva, 1989.

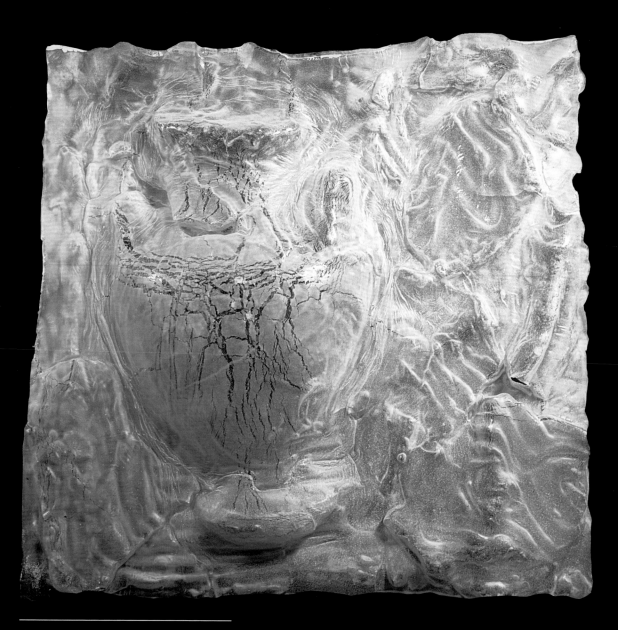

120. *The Sketch*
Lidiya Fomina and Timur Sazhin, 1989.

Catalog

1) *Kumgan* (Ewer)

Izmailovo, workshop master, Indrik Lerin, late 17th century
H. 21 cm

Colorless glass, blown, molded diamond pattern.

State History Museum, no. 41047/3075 st. Gift of N. I. Bulychev, 1903.

Kumgan is a word of Oriental origin. In the 17th and 18th centuries, it was applied in Russia to pitchers with spouts used to hold *kvass*, a weak homemade beer. The spout of this *kumgan* is in the shape of a ram's head—a motif that came to glassmaking from Russian ceramics. Three-dimensional figures of animals were also used on beakers and goblets.

Bibliography: Asharina (1971), p. 73; Asharina (1978), p. 23.

2) Beaker

Yamburg, about 1710–1720
H. 10.5 cm

Colorless glass, blown, engraved, inscribed "Vivat [Long live] Czar Peter Alekseevich," with Russia's state emblem: a double-headed eagle under three crowns, with Saint George on its breast.

State Hermitage, ERS 239. Received in 1941; previously kept in the Memorial Gallery of Peter the Great at the Academy of Sciences in St. Petersburg.

This beaker was engraved in honor of Peter the Great (1672–1725). From 1682 to 1721, he held the title of Czar Peter Alekseevich, and he became the first Russian emperor in 1721. He is known for his wide-ranging reforms and for his outstanding political and military leadership. In 1703, he founded St. Petersburg, and he moved the state capital there from Moscow in 1712. The double-headed eagle and the archaic letters point to the rather early date of the beaker. It may have been engraved by Johann Mennart, who was employed at Yamburg from 1713 to 1723.

Bibliography: O. Liven (1901), p. 14; Shelkovnikov (1960), fig. 2.

3) Covered Goblet

Yamburg, 1730–1740
H. 38 cm

Colorless glass, blown, faceted, engraved. The round medallion framed by two branches contains a profile portrait of Empress Anna Ivanovna; the other medallion contains the Russian emblem.

State History Museum, no. 62958/1991. Received in 1928 from the Institute of the Agricultural Economy.

Anna Ivanovna, niece of Peter the Great, was the Russian empress from 1730 to 1740. Her image on the silver rubles of 1730–1736 served as the design source for this portrait. However, the image on the goblet is very sketchy; the engraver failed to achieve a portrait likeness. Significantly, the portraits of Ioann Antonovich (ca. 1740–1741) and Elizabeth Petrovna were engraved on some goblets in a similar manner. This suggests that the creator of these portraits worked in the 1730s and 1740s.

Bibliography: Asharina (1980), p. 55.

4) Covered Goblet

St. Petersburg, mid-18th century
H. 38 cm

Colorless glass, blown, faceted, engraved, gilded, nielloed; in the circular medallions, the monogram of Elizabeth Petrovna and the Russian emblem.

State History Museum, no. 41174/1575. Received in 1902 from V. M. Dubrovsky.

Elizabeth Petrovna, daughter of Peter the Great and Catherine I, came to the Russian throne as the result of a palace coup on November 25, 1741. She was the Russian empress from 1741 to 1761.

This goblet is a typical example of products made by the St. Petersburg Glassworks. The monogram of the empress is known from the five-kopeck silver coins of 1755–1761 and the one-kopeck copper coins of 1755–1757. The decoration between the medallions is a modification of typical Bohemian engraved ornament of the early 18th century, which is of Renaissance origin.

Bibliography: Asharina (1978), p. 38; Asharina (1980), p. 66.

5) Beaker

St. Petersburg, 1750–1760
H. 15.5 cm

Colorless glass, blown, faceted, engraved. In three circular medallions framed with bands of polished circular facets, are a portrait of Elizabeth Petrovna, her monogram, and the Russian emblem.

State Hermitage ERS. 1988.

The source for the portrait of Empress Elizabeth Petrovna was a 1749 gold coin.

Bibliography: Catalog of State Hermitage (1984), no. 351.

6) Covered Goblet

St. Petersburg, 1750–1760
H. 28 cm

Colorless glass, blown, faceted, engraved, gilded, nielloed. Under a magnificent canopy supported by two putti there is a profile portrait of Empress Elizabeth Petrovna. The other cartouche contains the Russian emblem with the monogram "E.R." on the breast.

State History Museum, no. 33445/1573 st. Received in 1956 from museum stocks.

This goblet, typical both in form and size, reflects the high quality of cutting and engraving at the Imperial Factory. The lower part of the body is decorated with sculptural relief cutting, and the gilded engraving covering the goblet is marked by finesse and thoroughness of execution. Portraits of Elizabeth Petrovna with the splendid Baroque framework of an ermine mantle often appeared on goblets made at the St. Petersburg Glassworks, although one fully analogous to this engraving has not been found. Gilding and nielloing were used on the goblet to reproduce the hairdo of the empress; for some time, she either had her blond hair dyed black or wore a black wig.

7) Goblet

Glassworks in the village of Naziya, engraved in St. Petersburg, 1770–1780
H. 20 cm

Colorless glass, blown, faceted, engraved. The rocaille cartouche shows Catherine II with the trappings of imperial power. In the rays are the "all-seeing eye," two standards, the monogram of Catherine II, and the Russian emblem.

State Hermitage, ERS 3220. Acquired in 1984.

Catherine II ("the Great"), née Princess Sophia Frederica Anhalt Zerbst (1729–1796), was the wife of Emperor Peter III, who ascended to the throne in 1761. As the result of a palace coup in 1762, she reigned as empress until 1796.

8) Covered Goblet

Glassworks in the village of Naziya, engraved in St. Petersburg, 1770–1780
H. 32 cm

Colorless glass, blown, faceted, engraved. The allegorical composition shows two tritons pulling Neptune on a sea shell; over his head is a portrait of Catherine II. A battle involving two ships is also shown.

State History Museum, no. 1231-shch/1689. Received in 1905 as part of the P. I. Shchukin collection donated to the museum.

Pyotr Ivanovich Shchukin (1853–1912), a Moscow textile industrialist, collector, and art patron, collected books, documents, coins, and pictorial and applied art works associated with Russian history. He erected a special building on Malaya Gruzinskaya Street to house his enormous collection. In 1905, he donated this collection of more than 30,000 items to the Russian Historical Museum.

The decoration on this goblet is linked with the events of the first Russo-Turkish War (1768–1774). Turkey, which started the war, was defeated, and Russia firmly established its presence on the Black Sea coast. The allegory signifies that Catherine II became the ruler of the seas. The subject may have been borrowed from the repertoire of the numerous festivities with fireworks displays that were held in St. Petersburg to mark military victories. The portrait of Catherine II reproduced on the goblet was minted on Russian coins until 1777.

Bibliography: Asharina (1980), p. 66.

9) Covered Goblet

Vasily Maltsov's glassworks, mid-18th century; engraved by Stepan Lagutin
H. 27 cm

Colorless glass, blown, faceted, engraved, gilded. A medallion on the bowl, surrounded by a cartouche, shows a reindeer wounded by an arrow, fleeing from the castle. Inscribed: "A Flight from Illness."

State History Museum, no. 99411/1485. Received in 1956 from museum stocks.

The medallion bears the engraved emblem no. 587 from the collection *Symbols and Emblems*, published in Amsterdam in 1705 and ordered by Peter the Great. It contained 839 emblems, each with an explanation in Latin, French, German, English, and Russian. This set was a reprint of German collections from the late 17th century. The emblem on the goblet is explained by the inscription "A Flight from Illness," which was changed in later editions to "Illness Is the Reason for My Flight."

Bibliography: Asharina (1978), p. 40; Asharina (1980), p. 71.

10) Figural Bear-Bottle

Russia, unknown glassworks, first half of 18th century
H. 31 cm

Transparent green glass, blown.

State History Museum, no. 42567/-B-/1912. Received in 1905 as part of a large collection donated by A. P. Bakhrushin. Alexei Petrovich Bakhrushin (1853–1904), a prominent Moscow industrialist, booklover, and collector, bequeathed to the museum his huge library and collection consisting of documents, maps, coins, manuscripts, engravings, paintings, and household items pertaining to the history of the Russian state since ancient times.

At some glassworks, small numbers of figural vessels were made by craftsmen for themselves. It is known, for example, that at the Maltsovs' glassworks masters were able to work one day a week on their own work to upgrade their skills. Making a vessel in the shape of a bear may have been prompted by figural bottles, large numbers of which were blown by small Ukrainian workshops in the 17th–19th centuries. Ukrainian masters were often invited to Russian glassworks to work as blowers and to be in charge of mixing the batch. However, there is a substantial difference between the Russian and Ukrainian bear-vessels. Ukrainian bears were blown of very thin and fragile colorless or violet glass, while Russian ones were made of hard bottle-green glass. Masters also had different approaches to models. The Ukrainians conveyed the "mythological" basis of the image, while the Russian glass bears were more realistic.

Bibliography: Asharina (1974), p. 49.

11) Bottle

Russia, unknown private glassworks, first half of 18th century
H. 25 cm

Transparent green glass, blown, opaque red, yellow, and green enameled decoration. The decoration is a figure of a lion framed by two branches and the inscription "Lion."

State History Museum, no. 56994/1261 st. Purchased from Rasul Magomedov in 1925.

This bottle, which holds a quarter of a bucket, belongs to a group that was widespread in the 18th century. The depiction of lions with colored tails dates back to the Russian art traditions of Kiev Rus (12th–14th centuries), when the lion was one of the feudal symbols. In the 17th century, Russian art returned to this image, which later became part of urban and peasant folklore.

Bibliography: Asharina (1978), p. 54.

12) Jug

Russia, unknown glassworks, second half of 18th century
H. 27 cm

Transparent green glass, blown, painted with opaque red, pale blue, yellow, and white enameled decoration. The design is a lady holding a goblet, a gentleman, and a violinist.

State History Museum, no. 32700/1222 st. Purchased from F. M. Chelyshkin in 1895.

Such jugs, intended for *kvass*, were often called *kvassniks*. Similar holiday scenes were reproduced on *shtofs* (vodka flasks), bottles, and small casks in the first half of the 18th century. These dynamic scenes were often supplemented with such details as dancing, carriage-riding, and pictures of fistfights.

Bibliography: Asharina (1974), p. 48; Asharina (1978), p. 53.

13) Mosaic Portrait of Pyotr Ivanovich Shuvalov
Mikhail Lomonosov's workshop, 1758; tesserae from Lomonosov's Ust' Ruditsa works (made by Matvey Vasilyev, Yefim Melnikov, and Ignat Petrov)
57 x 45 cm

Mosaic picture. Shuvalov is depicted to the waist, wearing a green uniform with Orders of Saint Andrew the First Called and the White Eagle.

State Hermitage, ERKm 675. Received in the 1930s from the State Museum Fund.

Pyotr Ivanovich Shuvalov (1711–1762), was a count, general field marshal, senator, and participant in the 1741 palace coup that brought Elizabeth Petrovna to the throne. During her reign, he was virtually the head of state. He was also one of the leaders of the Russian army in the Seven-Years War (1756–1763).

Bibliography: N. Ye Makarenko (1917), p. 74; Makarov (1949), pp. 14 and 26; Makarov (1950), pp. 136–139; Catalog of State Hermitage (1979), p. 98; Catalog of State Hermitage (1984), p. 86.

14) Icon, *Our Lady of Cyprus*
Russia, late 18th century
32 x 26.5 cm

Board, tempera; the covering has bugle beads, spangles, and foil sewn on cloth.

State History Museum, no. 20171/90—bis 1216. Purchased from F. Chelyshkin in 1897.

15) Covered Mug
Imperial Glassworks, late 18th century
H. 10.5 cm

Transparent dark green (chrome) glass, blown, cut, gilded. On a medallion, the monogram "J.A.S." appears under a crown.

State History Museum, no. 76092/36 st. Received in 1936 from the study room of artistic design at Moscow State University.

16) Decanter with Stopper
Imperial Glassworks, late 18th or early 19th century
H. 23.5 cm

Scarlet (gold ruby) glass, blown, cut, gilded. The stylized ornament is arranged in five tiers. The round medallion contains the monogram "R.D.C." beneath a princely crown.

State History Museum, no. 97339/1125 st. Received in 1961 from museum stocks.

Bibliography: Asharina (1981).

17) Covered Goblet
Imperial Glassworks, late 18th or early 19th century
H. 21 cm

Transparent dark blue (cobalt) glass, blown, cut, gilded. One medallion shows a landscape and monogram "L.P." in Cyrillic characters framed by palm and laurel branches; the other medallion contains the Latin monogram "P.P."

State History Museum, no. 2117—shch/1881 st. Received in 1905 as part of P. I. Shchukin's collection.

Bibliography: Asharina (1978), p. 62.

18) Mug with Landscape
Imperial Glassworks, end of 18th century
H. 8.5 cm

Opaque white glass, blown, enameled, gilded.

State History Museum, no. 674 cm. Received in 1905 as part of P. I. Shchukin's collection.

Bibliography: Asharina (1978), N 44.

19) Easter Egg with Landscape
Imperial Glassworks, end of 18th century
H. 5.5 cm

Opaque white glass, blown, enameled, gilded.

State History Museum, no. 64015/6628 cm. Received in 1928 from museum fund.

20) Discus with Star
Imperial Glassworks, early 19th century
H. (discus) 11 cm

Opal white glass, blown, painted, enameled, gilded.

State Russian Museum, nos. St. 333, St. 336.

The discus bears the pictures of the infant Jesus, a dove, and God, with inscriptions, cherubim, other angels, and figures on bended knees. The inscriptions on the side read, "In the earth are the sins of this world" and "Behold the Lamb of God."

The star depicts St. Gregory the Theologian, St. Nicholas, and St. John the Golden-mouthed, accompanied by inscriptions.

The discus, a component of the Orthodox church ritual, is a dish on a tray containing communion bread. The star, which appears on the discus to prevent the cover from touching the bread, consists of two flat arches linked crosswise at the top.

21) Covered Beaker

Bakhmetiev's glassworks, late 18th or early 19th century

H. 18.5 cm

Colorless glass, blown, cut, gilded, silvered. The lid and upper part of the body bear crossed floral garlands. The oval medallion (under a nobleman's crown) and princely mantle depicts the Osnobishin family's armorial emblem.

State History Museum, no. 2763 st. Received in 1905 as part of P. I. Shchukin's collection.

The Osnobishins are a noble Russian family. Since 1423, the family lived in Vladimir, Saratov, Tambov, and Penza. The emblem is not listed in the published collection of emblems and coats of arms. The elements of the emblem suggest that its owner came from the line of the princes of Smolensk and that the family later lost its title.

Bibliography: Asharina (1978), p. 69.

22) Wineglass

Bakhmetiev's glassworks, 1795

Alexander Vershinin (?)

H. 11 cm

Transparent violet (manganese) glass, blown, gilded. The monogram "A.P." beneath a princely crown appears in a circular medallion, with two bands of ornament. At the rim is a border of oak leaves; a band of stars is at the bottom of the bowl.

State History Museum, no. 8608—shch/2107 st. Received in 1905 as part of P. I. Shchukin's collection.

The monogram refers to Alexander Pavlovich (1777–1825), son of Emperor Paul I, who ruled as Emperor Alexander I from 1801 to 1825.

Bibliography: Asharina (1978), p. 61.

23) *Shtof* (Vodka Bottle)

F. G. Orlov's glassworks, 1796–1801

H. 24 cm

Transparent dark blue (cobalt) glass, blown, white enameling. On one broad side is the double-headed Russian eagle with the monogram "P I" (Paul I) on its breast. Two sides bear stylized plant designs.

State Hermitage, ERS 571. Received in 1941 from the State Museum of Ethnography.

The monogram refers to Czar Paul I (r. 1796–1801).

Bibliography: Catalog of State Hermitage (1987), no. 536.

24) Cup and Saucer

F. G. Orlov's glassworks, late 18th century

H. (cup) 3.5 cm, D. (saucer) 11.5 cm

Colorless glass, blown, white enameling. Floral garlands fastened with bows.

State History Museum, no. 54097/3811 st. Received in 1922 from the museum fund.

25) Decanter with Four Compartments

Imperial Glassworks, late 18th or early 19th century

H. 28 cm

Colorless glass, blown, opal glass stripes, gilded; gilded bronze mounts. The decanter has four compartments for different liquors, separated by internal partitions. The monogram "S.D." under a crown is repeated on each section in round medallions.

State History Museum, no. 88247/712 st. Received in 1956 from the museum fund.

26) Pieces from the "Orlov" Service (Decanter, Three Wineglasses, and a Champagne Glass)

Imperial Glassworks, late 18th or early 19th century

H. (taller decanter) 28.5 cm

Colorless glass, blown, cut, gilded. Circular medallions contain the monogram "AO."

State Hermitage, ERS 712, 665, 615, 637, 596. Received in 1919 from the palace of the counts Bobrinsky; ex coll. Ivan Davidovich Orlov.

Catalog of State Hermitage (1983–1984), nos. 122–124.

Part of this service is housed in the State Russian Museum. One of the decanters in the State Hermitage bears the label "To Varvara Davidovna in memory of her great-grandfather Alexei Petrovich Orlov (Major General, Commander of the Life Guards Cossack Regiment)."

Bibliography: Kachalov (1956), st. 87; Dubova (1984), pp. 18 and 19; Malinina (1985), p. 102.

27) Double-Walled Tumbler
N. A. Bakhmetiev's glassworks, early 1800s
H. 12.5 cm

Colorless glass, blown, cut, gilded, silvered, enameled. Between the walls of the tumbler are straw, paper, and grass, depicting a rural landscape with people riding in a boat.

State History Museum, no. 78092/38 st. Received in 1936 from the study room of artistic design at Moscow State University.

Alexander Petrovich Vershinin, master at Bakhmetiev's glassworks, was famous for his double-walled tumblers. Eight such tumblers are known today. In technique, manner of execution, and ornamentation, this tumbler is very similar to a signed tumbler, made by Vershinin and dated 1802, from the museum collection at the glassworks.

28) Tripod Vase
Andrei Nikiforovich Voronikhin, Imperial Glassworks, early 1800s
H. 66 cm

Colorless glass, blown, cut, ground; cast, chased, engraved, and gilded bronze mounts. Vase is in the shape of a bowl with scalloped edge resting on a tripod consisting of three eagle-headed herms of glass and bronze.

State Hermitage, ERS 2682. From the private apartment of Empress Maria Feodorovna in the Winter Palace.

A pair to this vase is also in the collection of the State Hermitage.

29) Tripod Vase
Ivan Alekseevich Ivanov, Imperial Glassworks, 1820–1830
H. 48.5 cm

Colorless glass, blown, cut, engraved; chased and gilded bronze mounts.

State Hermitage, ERS 2689 A, B. From the main holdings of the museum.

Three similar vases are also in the collection of the State Hermitage.

30) Covered Goblet with Victory
Imperial Glassworks, after 1814
H. 23 cm

Colorless glass, blown, cut, gilded, applied opal glass medallion with polychrome enameled decoration. Victory with trumpet and garland hovers over a map of Europe showing Borodino, Tarutino, Malyy Yaroslavets, Lützen, Baruzzino, Dresden, Kulm, Leipzig, Brienne, Areis, and Paris. Under the picture is the monogram "F.D.D."

State History Museum, no. 13707—shch/1764 st. Received in 1905 as part of P. I. Shchukin's collection.

This goblet commemorates the 1812 Patriotic War and the Russian army's European campaigns in 1813–1814. The war was started when Napoleon invaded Russia on June 12, 1812. That invasion was repulsed, and by January 1813 the French army had been driven out of Russia. In 1813 and 1814, the Russian army, together with allied forces, scored a number of victories, and it entered Paris on March 19, 1814. Napoleon was forced to abdicate. The map shows the war's most important battles involving Russian troops. Significantly, the battle of Waterloo (June 6, 1815) is not shown on the map because the Russians' involvement in the war ended with the fall of Paris.

31) Covered Mug
Imperial Glassworks, 1820–1830
H. 15.5 cm

Transparent dark green (chrome) glass, blown, cut, gilded. The circular medallion bears a profile portrait. Inscribed "Count Wittgenstein."

State History Museum, no. 13726—shch/2811 st. Received in 1905 as part of P. I. Shchukin's collection.

Pyotr Khristianovich Wittgenstein (1768–1849) was a count, general of cavalry, and participant in the war against Napoleon in 1805–1807. He was one of the prominent army leaders in the 1812 Patriotic War and the 1813–1814 European campaigns. In 1812, he commanded a corps in St. Petersburg; a year later, he took part in the battles at Dresden and Leipzig. The portrait was made from an engraving by I. Chessky.

32) Plate, *Peace to Europe*
Imperial Glassworks, 1830–1840; engraved by J. Gube from the original design by Fyodor Tolstoy
D. 24 cm

Colorless glass, blown, cut; the center of the plate bears an engraved medallion of yellow "silver stain." Engraved allegorical composition, inscribed "Peace to Europe" and the date 1815.

State History Museum, no. 13728—shch/3643 st. Received in 1905 as part of P. I. Shchukin's collection.

Fyodor Petrovich Tolstoy (1783–1873) was a Russian medal maker, sculptor, painter, and graphic artist. From 1814 to 1836, he made 21 medallions commemorating the 1812 Patriotic War and the Russian army's European campaigns. This engraving may have been made from plaster of Paris castings of medals produced in 1829 or bronze medals issued by the St. Petersburg Mint, from dies prepared by A. Klepikov and A. Lyalin in the 1830s. The allegorical composition is devoted to the 1815 Vienna Congress, which concluded the war against Napoleon.

Bibliography: Tatevosova (1979), p. 19.

33) Medallion, *The Battle of Borodino*
(after a medallion by Fyodor Tolstoy)
Imperial Glassworks, 1830–1840
W. 21 cm

Colorless glass, cut, encased sulphide. Inside the octagonal glass form is a circular sulphide medallion with a molded allegorical relief. The inscription identifies the scene as "The Battle of Borodino 1812" and in smaller letters is the signature "Invented and Cut by Count Fyodor Tolstoy. 1817."

State History Museum, no. 42567/4490 st. Received in 1905 as part of the Bakhrushin collection.

34) Vase
Imperial Glassworks, 1830–1840
H. 56 cm

Colorless glass with inner scarlet (gold ruby) layer, blown, cut; chased and gilded bronze mounts. The glass parts were assembled using bronze elements; bronze mascarons support the heavy handles; the body of the vase is supported by bronze stem resting on a glass pedestal and bronze foot.

State History Museum, no. 83156/4724 st. Received in 1950 from the state holdings.

Bibliography: Shelkovnikov (1969), p. 139; Asharina (1978), p. 80.

35) Footed Bowl
Imperial Glassworks, first third of 19th century
H. 18 cm

Scarlet (gold ruby) glass, blown, cut; cast, chased, and gilded mounts. Bronze handles in the shape of eagles; the base is decorated with floral ornaments.

State Hermitage, ERS 2717. From the main collection of the Hermitage; previously, this object was among the personal belongings of Emperor Nicholas I and his wife in the Winter Palace.

36) Footed Bowl
Imperial Glassworks, 1830–1840
H. 16 cm

Pink opalescent glass, blown, cut; malachite mosaic; cast and engraved gilded bronze mounts.

State Hermitage, ERS 2565. Received in 1927.

Malachite, a traditional Russian stone mined in the Ural Mountains, was used lavishly during the first half of the 19th century to decorate palaces, ceremonial halls, and applied art works.

Bibliography: Voronov and Dubova (1984), p. 53.

37) Decanter with Stopper
Imperial Glassworks, second quarter of 19th century
H. 18 cm

Three layers of glass (green on white on red), blown, cut. Ornamented with cut, multicolored squares.

State Hermitage, ERS 1426 A, B. Received in 1941; ex coll. F. M. Plyushkin.

F. M. Plyushkin, a major pre-revolutionary collector of Russian antiques, lived in Pskov.

38) Decanter with Stopper
Imperial Glassworks, second half of 19th century
H. 21.5 cm

Colorless glass, blown, encrusted enameled gold foil. The four oval medallions on the decanter's sides and in the top of the stopper encase polychrome enameled gold foil floral bouquets.

State Hermitage, ERS 2533. Acquired in 1965.

39) Goblet
Dyat'kovo Crystal Works, 1860–1870
H. 14 cm

Colorless glass, blown, cut, with encrusted coat of arms of colored enamel on gold and silver foil. The coat of arms is that of the noble family of the Kolokoltsovs. The family of the Kolokoltsovs in the Saratov region was widely known for its workshop manned by serfs. The famous Kolokoltsov shawls were made there in the first half of the 19th century.

State History Museum, no. 54679/1853 st. Received in 1923 from the First Proletarian Museum.

The technique of encrusting glass with enameled gold foil devices was borrowed from the banquet services of the Imperial Glassworks. A Dyat'kovo Crystal Works vase in the collection of the State History Museum was also made by this method. According to contemporary accounts, entire iconostases of churches in the villages of Dyat'kovo and Lyudionov were made with "false foil."

40) Chalice
Unknown Russian glassworks, second quarter of 19th century
H. 37 cm

Colorless glass, blown, cut, gilded, silvered, and transparent colored enameling. Inscribed: "Partake of the Body of Christ, receive the source of the immortal." In the medallions: Jesus, the Virgin (Mary), John the Baptist, and three crosses.

State History Museum, no. 80275/4356 st. Received in 1939 from the State Theater Museum.

The chalice, the cup used in the sacrament of the Eucharist, always bears the images of our Lord, the Virgin (Mary), and John the Baptist.

41) Seven Pieces of the "Gothic" Service (Fruit Compote, Decanter with Stopper, Dessert Plate and Dish, *Römer*, and Two Wineglasses)
Imperial Glassworks (Ivan Alekseevich Ivanov?), second quarter of the 19th century
H. (fruit compote) 40 cm

Colorless glass, blown, with blue overlay, green and brilliant red (gold ruby) glass, cut.

State History Museum, 62542/502, 496, 506, 500, 493 st; 106248/6424 st.

Fruit compote, decanter with stopper, dessert plate, creamer, and *Römer* received in 1928 from the Leningrad museum fund; two wineglasses acquired in 1985.

Bibliography: Kachalov (1959), p. 243; Shelkovnikov (1969), p. 166; Asharina (1978), p. 181; Malinina (1985), p. 103.

42) Covered Mug
Maltsovs' glassworks, second quarter of 19th century
H. 18.5 cm

Colorless glass with dark red (copper ruby) overlay, blown, cut.

State History Museum, no. 81202/4563 st. Received in 1943.

Dark cherry-colored glass, colored with copper compounds ("copper ruby"), appeared much later than "gold ruby." Its rarity is evident from an archival document (dated 1841) in which an anonymous correspondent wrote from Prague to St. Petersburg that the chemist Egermann of Haida was ready to sell the formula for copper ruby glass for 300 talers. However, this deal did not materialize because such glass was already made at Russian glassworks. The *Journal of Industry and Trade* in 1837 documents that copper ruby glass was then made at the Maltsov, Orlov, and Bakhmetiev glassworks.

Bibliography: Asharina (1978), p. 98.

43) Decanter with Stopper
Gus Crystal Works, mid-19th century
H. 32 cm

Transparent brilliant green (uranium) glass, blown, cut. Broad panel cutting on the sides, with cut oval projecting pads forming the feet.

Crystal Museum in the city of Gus' Khrustal'nyy. (V-30000/17, from the specimen collection of the glassworks.)

Russian production of uranium glass began in the early 1840s. There were two types of uranium glass: "green" and "yellow." "Uranium green" signified an intense green glass, while "yellow" meant opalescent greenish-yellow glass. The expressive possibilities of this glass were particularly well revealed in thick-walled vessels, and Russian masters never spared material in making uranium glass objects. In the middle of the 19th century, these objects were made at the Imperial and Maltsov glassworks. After 1850, the latter factory produced collections of "specimens," enabling a large number of its glass objects to be preserved. Those collections served as the basis for museums now open to the public.

44) Perfume Bottle
Imperial Glassworks, second quarter of 19th century
H. 15.5 cm

Opaque red Hyalith glass, blown, cut, gilded, silvered.

State Hermitage, ERS 1500 a, b. Received in 1941 from the State Museum of Ethnography.

45) Vase
Imperial Glassworks, second half of 19th century
H. 38.5 cm

Opalescent white glass, blown, blue enameling, gilded, silvered. The ornamentation derives from medieval Iranian phytomorphic motifs.

State Hermitage, ERS 228. From the Department of Western European Art of the Hermitage; ex coll. Museum of the Baron Stieglitz School of Technical Drawing.

In 1876, Baron A. L. Stieglitz founded a state art school in St. Petersburg to train teachers of drawing and supervisors of applied art. The school had a library and a museum established by A. A. Polovtsov. In the late 1920s and 1930s, works of art from that museum were given to various museums in Leningrad. After World War II, the school was refounded; it is now called the Mukhina Higher School of Industrial Design.

46) Vase
Imperial Glassworks, 1870–1880
H. 34 cm

Opaque pale greenish-white glass, blown, polychrome enameled, gilded. Ornamentation in "Oriental" style. Monogram on the bottom: "A II."

State Hermitage, ERS 2429. From the Museum of the Baron Stieglitz School of Technical Drawing.

The monogram refers to Czar Alexander II (r. 1855–1881).

Bibliography: Malinina (1983), p. 9.

47) Vase
Imperial Glassworks, second half of 19th century
H. 37 cm

Opal and cobalt blue glass, blown, gilded; cast, chased, and engraved bronze mounts. The form resembles that of traditional Chinese porcelain vases.

State Hermitage, ERS 2495 a, 2496 b. From the main holdings of the museum.

This vase belonged to the countess Yelena Georgievna, a member of a czar's family. She was an owner of the Chinese palace in Oranienbaum in the second half of the 19th century.

Bibliography: Shelkovnikov (1964), fig. 24; Shelkovnikov (1969), fig. 93.

48) Vase
Imperial Glassworks, 1880–1890
H. 29 cm

Smoky and colorless glass, blown, cut, transparent orange and blue enamels, gilded. Two birds are shown surrounded by branches with orange leaves and sky blue flowers; one is in a round medallion, and the other is in a rectangular reserve. On the bottom is the monogram "A III."

State History Museum, no. 81202/4599 st. Received in 1943.

The monogram refers to Czar Alexander III (r. 1881–1894)

Bibliography: Asharina (1978), p. 103.

49) Jug
Gus Crystal Works, about 1893
H. 17 cm

Colorless glass, blown, overall silvering with scenes of Oriental musicians.

The Crystal Museum in the city of Gus' Khrustal'nyy. (V-30000/609, from the specimen collection of the glassworks.)

Similar silver-covered items with incised patterns in the "Persian" style were supplied by the Gus Crystal Works to the Chicago worlds's fair in 1893. They were intended for the Eastern market, where many of the factory's products were sold.

50) Covered Vase
Imperial Glassworks (Victor Alexandrovich Hartmann?), 1870–1880
H. 24.5 cm

Transparent dark blue (cobalt) glass, blown, polychrome enameling. The vase is in the form of pottery milk jugs used by peasants; the ornamentation derives from Russian folk embroidery. Monogram on the bottom: "A II."

State Hermitage, ERS 2426 a, b. Received from the Museum of the Baron Stieglitz School of Technical Drawing.

The monogram refers to Czar Alexander II (r. 1855–1881).

Bibliography: Shelkovnikov (1964), fig. 4; Catalog of State Hermitage (1964), fig. 76; Malinina and Sapunov (1989).

51) Decanter with Stopper
Imperial Glassworks (Victor Alexandrovich Hartmann?), 1870–1880
H. 25.5 cm

Colorless glass, blown, decorated in polychrome enamels. Decorated with three heads of horses cut from glass and enameled.

State Hermitage, ERS-1390 a, b. From the State Museum Fund.

Bibliography: Shelkovnikov (1959), p. 69; Shelkovnikov (1969), fig. 103; Catalog of State Hermitage (1964), fig. 75; Shelkovnikov (1989), fig. 22.

52) Covered Bowl and Plate from Service of the Princes Golitsyn
Imperial Glassworks, 1860–1880
H. 14 cm; D. 21 cm

Transparent dark red (gold ruby) glass, blown, cut, gilded. Decorated with the princes' coat of arms, plant motifs, and rosettes in circles.

State Hermitage, ERS-1743 a, b, c. Received in 1941 from the State Museum of Ethnography.

The Golitsyns were a noble family descended from the grand duke of Lithuania, Gedimin, whose son Gleb (d. 1348) was prince of Novgorod, Ladoga, and Orekhov. Many outstanding Russian statesmen, generals, writers, and scientists came from the Golitsyn family.

53) *Bratina*
Yelizaveta Boem, Dyat'kovo Crystal Works, 1875–1885
H. 17.5 cm

Colorless glass, blown, with gold luster, opaque polychrome enamel. Inscribed under the edge: "Step aside, man, or I'll pour it on you." On the bottom, trademark "MPTT Dyat'kovo Crystal Works" in a circle around a double-headed eagle.

State History Museum, no. 42567-B/3782 st. Received in 1905 as part of A. P. Bakhrushin's collection.

The first written mention of the *bratina*, a traditional "toast bowl" intended for communal drinking, dates to the 16th century. Wood, copper, and silver *bratinas* became widespread in the 17th century. Most of them were richly ornamented with paintings, chasing, engraving, or enameling. On the upper edge, there was usually an inscription wishing good health to those who drank from the bowl. This *bratina*, a reproduction of a 17th-century silver bowl with polychrome enamel, is a rare example of 19th-century glass objects bearing the trademark of the Dyat'kovo Crystal Works. The factory, founded by Marya Maltsova in 1796, later belonged to Ivan Akimovich and Sergei Ivanovich Maltsov. From 1875 to 1885, it was part of the Maltsov industrial and trade company; the trademark on the *bratina* dates to that period.

Bibliography: Shelkovnikov (1969), p. 178; Asharina (1978), p. 100; Asharina (1988), p. 263.

54) Part of Service for Vodka (*Shtof*, Four Glasses, and Tray)
Yelizaveta Boem, Dyat'kovo Crystal Works, 1897
H. (*shtof*)24 cm; D. (tray) 40 cm

Transparent green glass, blown, opaque black and orange enameling, showing frolicking devils. Inscribed on tray and *shtof*:
"Hello, little glasses, how are you getting on? Waiting for me? Drink, drink, and you'll see devils."
"Wine! Hey, my dear! Flow into my throat, my dear sun."
"The first is what I don't drink, the second is what I don't like, and the third is what I've already drunk!"
"They got tight and had a fight. After a sound sleep they drank the morning after and made up."
Signature under inscription: "Yeliz. Boem 1897."
Inscribed on glasses:
"The first glass for making merry"
"The second glass for making merry"
"The third glass for ardor"
"Ancient customs are quite clear, let us drink another, dear."

State History Museum, nos. 81202/4602–4607 st. Received in 1943.

Bibliography: Price List (1903), p. 116; Asharina (1981), p. 40; Asharina (1988), p. 263.

55) Vase
Imperial Glassworks, 1880–1890
H. 23.2 cm

Colorless glass, blown, yellow stain, engraved, cut. The design shows putti amid branches and flowers.

State Hermitage, ERS 2423; this object was among the personal belongings of Emperor Nicholas II and his wife in the Winter Palace.

Nicholas II (1868–1918) was Russia's Emperor from 1894 to 1917.

Bibliography: Catalog of State Hermitage (1989), N 78.

56) Covered Goblet
Gus Crystal Works, end of 19th century
H. 26 cm

Colorless glass, blown, relief cutting of palmettes and volutes.

Crystal Museum in the city of Gus' Khrustal'nyy. (V-30000/1051, from the specimen collection of the glassworks.)

57) Jug
Gus Crystal Works, early 20th century
H. 13 cm

Colorless glass, blown, cut, engraved.

Crystal Museum in the city of Gus' Khrustal'nyy. (V-30000/1565 st., from the specimen collection of the glassworks.)

Engraving was the chief method of decorating products at the Gus Crystal Works in the 18th century. When faceted glass became popular in the first half of the 19th century, engraving was used to decorate such inexpensive vessels as wineglasses, beakers, and decanters, many of which have survived. Engraving recaptured its prominence in the 1850s, and it was used to fill important orders. During his coronation in 1856, Alexander II received a tray engraved with the emblems of all the districts in the Vladimir region. The Travkin family were among the leading engravers at the Gus Crystal Works. One member of that family, Ivan Nikolayevich Travkin, may have produced this engraving.

Bibliography: Asharina (1988), p. 268.

58) Vase
Imperial China and Glass Works, 1899
H. 42 cm

Colorless glass, blown, engraved. Ovoid form with a little crown in the shape of a sea shell. The engraved decoration depicts the seabed and a swimming fish. Engraved on the bottom: monogram "N II" (Nicholas II) and the date.

State Hermitage, ERS 1976. Received from the State Museum of Ethnography; ex coll. Gatchina Palace.

Bibliography: Shelkovnikov (1969), pp. 176–177, fig. 106; Shelkovnikov (1967), p. 127, fig. 9; Catalog of State Hermitage (1974), N 208.

59) Vase
Imperial China and Glass works, 1898
H. 15.5 cm

Multi-layered glass (sky blue, green, opal), blown, etched, cameo-carved. The decoration is of leaves and a coiled snake. Engraved on the bottom: monogram "N II" and the date.

State Hermitage, ERS 1617. Received in 1941 from the State Museum of Ethnography.

The monogram refers to Czar Nicholas II (r. 1894–1917).

60) Vase
Gus Crystal Works, early 20th century
H. 42 cm

Two-layer opal and brown glass, blown, etched. Inscribed "YU.S.N.M. N-k Gus-Krust" (Yuri Stepanovich Nechayev-Maltsov, heir of Gus' Khrustal'nyy).

Crystal Museum in the city of Gus' Khrustal'nyy. (V-30000/1958, from the specimen collection of the glassworks.)

With the death of I. S. Maltsov in 1880, the family's control of the Gus Crystal Works was interrupted. From 1884 to 1894, the factory was operated by the government. In 1894, it became part of the joint-stock company of the Maltsov glassworks. Yu. S. Nechayev-Maltsov, a descendant of I. S. Maltsov, was the last owner of the glassworks.

61) Vase
Gus Crystal Works, early 20th century
H. 18 cm

Transparent green glass, iridized, threaded.

Crystal Museum in the city of Gus' Khrustal'nyy.
(V-30000/2022, from the specimen collection of the glassworks.)

62) Bowl
Gus Crystal Works, early 20th century
H. 19 cm

Transparent yellow glass with trailed and combed violet threading, iridized.

Crystal Museum in the city of Gus' Khrustal'nyy.
(V-30000/1994, from the specimen collection of the glassworks.)

63) Vase
Gus Crystal Works, early 20th century
H. 20 cm

Colorless glass with transparent green overlay, blown, cut, acid-etched.

Crystal Museum in the city of Gus' Khrustal'nyy.
(V-30000/2274, from the specimen collection of the glassworks.)

64) Vase
Gus Crystal Works, early 20th century
H. 28 cm

Colorless glass, blown, frosted, gilded, enameled, stained.

Crystal Museum in the city of Gus' Khrustal'nyy.
(V-30000/2275, from the specimen collection of the glassworks.)

65) Compote for Jam
Gus Crystal Works, early 20th century
H. 29 cm

Colorless and lilac glass, blown.

Crystal Museum in the city of Gus' Khrustal'nyy.
(V-30000/1195, from the specimen collection of the glassworks.)

66) Vase
Gus Crystal Works, early 20th century
H. 27 cm

Opaque red "jasper" glass, blown, faceted.

Crystal Museum in the city of Gus' Khrustal'nyy.
(V-30000/1919, from the specimen collection of the glassworks.)

67) Covered Jug and Tumbler
Gus Crystal Works, early 20th century
H. (jug) 42 cm

Colorless glass, blown, frosted, decorated with green, yellow, and transparent crimson enameling.

Crystal Museum in the city of Gus' Khrustal'nyy.
(V-30000/67, 2219, from the specimen collection of the glassworks.)

68) Four Pieces of a Table Service (Dessert Dish, Wineglass, Beaker, and Covered Compote for Jam)
Gus Crystal Works, early 20th century
H. (covered compote) 25 cm

Colorless glass, blown, engraved.

Crystal Museum in the city of Gus' Khrustal'nyy.
(V-30000/1325, 1321, 1320, 1331, from the specimen collection of the glassworks.)

In the late 19th and early 20th centuries, price lists were introduced at the Gus Crystal Works and at other factories belonging to the joint-stock company of the Maltsov glassworks. Using these lists, customers could order entire services or pieces from these sets. Each style and ornament had its own number, and this afforded the customer considerable freedom of choice. Despite the apparent diversity of forms and decoration, the compilers of the price lists actually used a relatively small number of elements. Products of colorless glass decorated with diamond cutting, guilloche, or engraving figured prominently in the lists, which differed little from one factory to another. This service, no. 107 on the price list, was decorated with a design called "decadent thread."

69) Three Pieces of a Table Service (Decanter, Beaker, and Wineglass)
Gus Crystal Works, early 20th century
H. (decanter) 34 cm

Colorless glass, blown, mechanical threading, cut.

Crystal Museum in the city of Gus' Khrustal'nyy.
(V-30000/1203, 1180, 1168, from the specimen collection of the glassworks.)

Bibliography: Kazakova (1973), p. 22.

70) Three Pieces of a Table Service (Two Wineglasses and Tumbler)
Gus Crystal Works, early 20th century
H. (taller wineglass) 18 cm

Colorless glass, blown, cut.

Crystal Museum in the city of Gus' Khrustal'nyy.
(V-30000/1000, 37, 1003, from the specimen collection of the glassworks.)

Bibliography: Prokof'ev (1970), p. 75.

71) Decanter
Unknown glassworks and C. Fabergé firm, Moscow, early 20th century
H. 19.5 cm

Colorless glass, blown, cut; cast, chased, and engraved silver mount.

State Hermitage, ERS 3217. Acquired in 1984.

"Russian stone" cutting, which was first used at the Imperial Glassworks in 1820–1830, was later employed at other private glasshouses in Russia.

72) Jug
Imperial China and Glass Works and C. Fabergé firm, late 19th or early 20th century
H. 26 cm

Colorless glass, blown, engraved; silver mount. Engraved scene of fish swimming amid seaweed.

State Hermitage, ERS 3187. Acquired in 1983.

73) Vase
Imperial China and Glass Works, 1897
H. 36.3 cm

Multicolored glass with crackle on inner surface, blown, mottled vertical stripes of yellow, green, sky blue, black, white, and colorless glass. Engraved on the bottom: monogram "N II" (Nicholas II) and the date.

State Hermitage, ERS 2998. From the Peterhof Palace Museum.

Bibliography: Catalog of State Hermitage (1974), no. 199.

74) Jug, *Five-Year Plan in Four Years*
Gus Crystal Works, about 1929–1932
H. 40 cm

Colorless glass, blown, frosted, enameled.

Crystal Museum in the city of Gus' Khrustal'nyy.
(No. 30000/2424, from the specimen collection of the glassworks.)

The first Five-Year Plan of USSR Economic Development, adopted in 1929, was designed to industrialize the country at a quick pace. Shortly thereafter, the slogan "Five-Year Plan in Four Years" was heard, and the plan was considered to have been fulfilled in 1932. Jugs of this form were made by the Gus Crystal Works from the early 1900s to the 1940s.

75) Vase with Soviet Emblems
Gus Crystal Works, 1937
H. 38 cm

Opal glass, blown, enameled. On the body: a five-pointed star containing a picture of the Savior's Tower in the Moscow Kremlin and the inscription "XX years." Commemorates the 20th anniversary of the 1917 Socialist Revolution.

Crystal Museum in the city of Gus' Khrustal'nyy.
(No. 30000/2287, from the specimen collection of the glassworks.)

76) Vase, *Sea Depths*
Gus Crystal Works, about 1939
H. 32 cm

Sky blue and colorless glass, blown, overlaid, etched. Fish decoration.

Crystal Museum in the city of Gus' Khrustal'nyy, no. 30000/2344.

This vase was probably made for the 1939 All-Union Agricultural Exhibition in Moscow.

77) Vase
Gus Crystal Works, about 1947
H. 32 cm

Colorless glass, blown, dark red (copper ruby) overlay, cut, etched.

Crystal Museum in the city of Gus' Khrustal'nyy, no. 30000/454.

This vase was probably made to commemorate Moscow's 800th anniversary, which was celebrated in 1947. The Savior's Tower in the Moscow Kremlin and the Intercession Cathedral, also known as the Cathedral of Saint Basil the Blessed (built in 1555–1556), are depicted on the sides.

78) **Wash Bowl and Pitcher**
Gus Crystal Works, late 1940s
D. (bowl) 43 cm

Colorless glass, blue overlay, blown, cut.

Crystal Museum in the city of Gus' Khrustal'nyy, no. L 30000/98, 4904.

79) **Vase,** *Aster*
Vera Ignatyevna Mukhina, 1940–1941
H. 18.8 cm

Transparent gray glass, blown, cut.

State Russian Museum, no. 2672.

Bibliography: Voronov and Dubova (1974), p. 103; Voronov (1981), p. 19.

80) *Torso*
Vera Ignatyevna Mukhina, 1940–1941, cast in 1949
H. 67 cm

Colorless glass, cast; wood base.

State Russian Museum, no. 235.

Bibliography: Kachalov (1959), p. 275; Voronov and Dubova (1984), p. 111.

81) **Vase**
Alexei Alexandrovich Uspensky, 1940
H. 46 cm

Colorless and milk-white glass, blown.

State Institute of Glass, Moscow, no. LD 41.

Bibliography: Kachalov (1959), fig. 267.

82) **Vase**
Gus Crystal Works, 1950–1960
H. 24 cm

Colorless and opalescent orange glass, blown, cut.

Crystal Museum in the city of Gus' Khrustal'nyy, no. 30000/3559.

83) **Vase,** *Outer Space*
Vladimir Alexandrovich Filatov, 1959
H. 19 cm

Transparent amber glass, blown, cut.

Crystal Museum in the city of Gus' Khrustal'nyy, no. 30000/2889.

Bibliography: Prokof'ev (1970), p. 111.

84) **Vase,** *Glassblowers*
Boris Alexandrovich Smirnov, 1961
H. 52 cm

Colorless glass, blown, sandblasted.

State History Museum, no. 6076 cm. Received in 1979 from Art Fund of RSFSR.

Bibliography: Batanova and Voronov (1964), fig. 44; Pavlinskaya (1980), p. 83.

85) **Vase,** *Electrification*
Helle Martinovna Põld, 1968
H. 26 cm

Colorless glass, blown, engraved.

State History Museum, no. 6056. 1978 gift to Leningrad.

Bibliography: Voronov and Rachuk (1973), p. 23.

86) **Troika**
Yuri Mikhailovich Byakov, 1968
H. 29.5 cm

Colorless glass, blown, sandblasted.

Museum of Leningrad art glass work, no. 14023.

Bibliography: Voronov and Dubova (1974), fig. 53.

87) **Vase,** *Neptune*
Aknuny Arkadyevich Astvatsaturyan, 1968
H. 32 cm

Transparent green and blue glass, blown, polished.

USSR Ministry of Culture, no. 167100.

Bibliography: Voronov and Rachuk (1973), fig. 22; Voronov and Dubova (1974), fig. 42; Rachuk (1982), fig. 3.

88) **Vase,** *Nests*
Victor Yakovlevich Shevchenko, 1968
H. 36 cm

Dark blue and cloudy white sulfide glass, blown, impressed.

Property of the artist.

Bibliography: Stepanyan (1978), fig. 32.

89) *Foma and Yeryoma*
Vladimir Vasilyevich Korneyev, 1967
H. 30 cm and 38.5 cm

Transparent red, green, and amber glass, blown.

Crystal Museum in the city of Gus' Khrustal'nyy, nos. 30000/2988, 2987.

Bibliography: Kazakova (1973), fig. 88.

90) *Man, Horse, Dog, Bird*
Boris Alexandrovich Smirnov, 1970
H. 37 cm

Colorless and opaque red, blue, and yellow glass, blown.

USSR Ministry of Culture, no. 49.

Bibliography: Pavlinskaya (1980), p. 100.

91) Vase, *Mars*
Dmitry Nikolayevich Shushkanov and Lyudmila Nikolayevna Shushkanova, 1973
H. 15.5 cm

Variegated colored glass, blown.

USSR Ministry of Culture, no. 73901.

Bibliography: Kantor (1981), fig. 113.

92) *Bee*
Irina Mikhailovna Marshumova, 1974
H. 18 cm

Colorless glass, lampworked.

USSR Ministry of Culture, no. pr. 86534.

93) *Dragonfly*
Irina Mikhailovna Marshumova, 1974
H. 27 cm

Colorless glass, lampworked.

USSR Ministry of Culture, no. pr. 86536.

94) *Venice*
Vladimir Petrovich Zhokhov, 1974
H. (tallest) 42 cm

Colorless glass, blown.

USSR Ministry of Culture, no. pr. 46.

Bibliography: Voronov (1981), fig. 205; Catalog: Riihimäki (1984), p. 7.

95) Vase, *Forest Ranges*
Yevgheny Ivanovich Rogov, 1971
H. 39 cm

Colorless glass, blown, engraved.

Crystal Museum in the city of Gus' Khrustal'nyy, no. 30000/3007.

Bibliography: Kazakova (1973), figs. 28 and 29.

96) *Minotaur*
Fidail Mulla Akhmetovich Ibragimov, 1968
H. 39 cm

Opaque black glass, blown, engraved.

State Museum of Ceramics and Kuskovo Estate, no. 3019 st.

Bibliography: Kazakova (1973), p. 155.

97) *He and She*
Yekaterina Vasilyevna Yanovskaya, 1970
D. 35 cm

Colorless glass with transparent red, green, and blue spots, blown, cut, engraved.

State History Museum, no. 107761(1-2)/6631, 6632 st. Received in 1989.

Bibliography: Voronov and Dubova (1974), fig. 26; Voronov and Rachuk (1973), figs. 17 and 18; Catalog: Yanovskaya (1980), fig. 25.

98) *The Arctic*
Vladimir Sergeyevich Muratov, 1974
H. 59 cm; D. 45 cm

Colorless glass, blown, cut, sandblasted, frosted.

Crystal Museum in the city of Gus' Khrustal'nyy, no. V-27100.

99) *Galatea*
Adolf Mikhailovich Ostroumov, 1974
H. 52.5 cm

Colorless glass, blown, sandblasted, frosted.

Museum of Leningrad art glass work, no. 16827.

Bibliography: Voronov and Dubova (1981), p. 194.

100) Vase, *Autumn*
Leida Oskarovna Jurgen, 1974
H. 19 cm

Transparent amber glass, blown, overlaid, cut.

Museum of Leningrad art glass work, no. 6301.

101) *Summer*
Galina Alexandrovna Antonova, 1975
H. (tallest) 38 cm

Opaque red and yellow, and transparent green glass, blown.

USSR Ministry of Culture, no. 80716.

Bibliography: Catalog: Antonova (1984), p. 15.

102) *Mountebanks*
Yuri Mikhailovich Manelis, 1978
H. (tallest) 40 cm

Colorless, opaque red, yellow, and orange, and transparent dark blue glass, blown.

Property of the artist.

Bibliography: Voronov (1981), fig. 91.

103) *Chuckotka*
Natal'ya Borisovna Tikhomirova, 1975
H. (tallest) 39 cm

Colorless glass, blown, cut.

Museum of Leningrad art glass works, nos. 15992, 15993, 16005.

Bibliography: Voronov and Dubova (1984), p. 265.

104) *A Wind of Wandering*
Vladimir Konstantinovich Pogrebnoy, 1978
H. (taller) 65 cm

Colorless glass, blown, sandblasted.

USSR Ministry of Culture, no. 91378.

Bibliography: Voronov (1981), p. 30; Catalog: Riihimäki (1984), p. 12.

105) *Dream*
Boris Fyodorov, 1981
D. (largest) 38 cm

Transparent gray glass, blown, engraved.

USSR Ministry of Culture, no. pr. 48.

Bibliography: Catalog: Riihimäki (1984), p. 11.

106) *Summer Garden*
Natal'ya Mikhailovna Goncharova, 1981
H. 35.5 cm

Colorless glass, blown, engraved, sandblasted.

Museum of Leningrad art glass work, no. 17734.

The Summer Garden in Leningrad was established in 1704.

107) *Listening to Stravinsky*
Ivan Vasilyevich Machnev, 1981
H. (tallest) 54 cm

Colorless glass, blown, cut.

USSR Ministry of Culture, no. pr. 3885.

Bibliography: Catalog: Riihimäki (1984), p. 33.

108) **Bowl,** *Inspiration*
Adolf Stepanovich Kurilov, 1982
D. 42.5 cm

Colorless glass, blown, cut, engraved, sandblasted.

Crystal Museum in the city of Gus' Khrustal'nyy, no. 30700.

109) *Self-Portrait in Space*
Lyubov Ivanovna Savelyeva, 1982
H. (tallest) 40 cm

Colorless and transparent blue glass, blown, enameled.

State History Museum, no. 106038/6404–6409. Received in 1985.

Bibliography: Catalog: Glass, Image, Space (1987), p. 41.

110) Dedicated to *Pirosmani*
Vladimir Ivanovich Kotov, 1984
H. (tallest) 33 cm

Opaque black glass, blown, enameled, sandblasted.

Property of the artist.

Niko Pirosmanishvili or Pirosmani (1862–1918) was a Georgian artist and self-taught Primitivist whose favorite motif in his paintings was Georgian feasts.

Bibliography: Catalog of State Hermitage (1989).

111) *India*
Dmitry Nikolayevich Shushkanov and Lyudmila Nikolayevna Shushkanova, 1984
H. (taller) 35.5 cm

Variegated opaque light blue and amber glass, blown.

USSR Ministry of Culture, no. 4478.

112) *And the Sky Is Full of Stars*
Natal'ya Vitaliyevna Uryadova, 1985
H. (taller) 24.2 cm

Transparent opalescent white optical glass, cut.

USSR Ministry of Culture, no. 3554.

113) *White Nights*
Alexander Alekseevich Ivanov, 1986
H. (taller) 50 cm

Transparent gray glass, blown, engraved.

Property of the artist.

Bibliography: Catalog: Glass, Image, Space (1987), p. 25.

114) My Muse
Svetlana Grigoryevna Ryazanova, 1984
H. 56 cm

Opaque white and yellow glass, mold-blown.

USSR Ministry of Culture, no. pr. 3677.

Bibliography: Catalog: Ryazanova (1984), p. 7.

115) Vases from The South
Vyacheslav Sergeevich Zaitzev, 1985
H. (taller) 38 cm

Transparent amber and green glass, blown, cut, sand-blasted

Crystal Museum in the city of Gus' Khrustal'nyy, no. 37072/1–2.

116) Vases, Pairs
Olga Ivanovna Kozlova, 1987
H. (taller) 32 cm

Colorless and transparent amber, amethyst, and red glass, blown, ground.

USSR Ministry of Culture, no. pr. 5279.

117) Emotion
Vladimir Ivanovich Kasatkin, 1987
D. 45 cm

Colorless and transparent amethyst glass, blown, cut, sandblasted.

Property of the artist.

Bibliography: Catalog: Farbglass (1989), fig. 10.

118) The Epoch
Vladimir Sergeyevich Muratov, 1987
H. 30 cm

Colorless glass with pink mottling, blown, sandblasted.

Property of the artist.

119) The Space-3
Lyubov Ivanovna Savelyeva, 1989
H. (tallest) 31 cm

Colorless glass, blown, enameled.

Property of the artist.

120) The Sketch
Lidiya Andreevna Fomina and Timur Petrovich Sazhin, 1989
64 x 61 cm

Translucent greenish-white glass, cast.

Property of the artist.

Biographical Sketches

Antonova, Galina Alexandrovna, Moscow (b. 1926). Merited Artist of RSFSR. Began studying at Moscow Institute of Applied and Decorative Art in 1947. Graduated from Mukhina Higher School of Industrial Design in Leningrad in 1953. Was employed at Moscow Integrated Works of Applied Art of Moscow Organization of the Artistic Foundation of RSFSR in 1959. Started teaching at Moscow Higher School of Industrial Design (Assistant Professor) in 1962. Began making her articles at the Dyat'kovo Crystal Works and the Lvov Ceramic and Sculptural Factory of the Artistic Foundation of the Ukrainian SSR in 1975. During business trips to Czechoslovakia made numerous articles at various glassworks. In 1970 started making glass articles for interior of various public buildings (jointly with S. Ryazanova and A. Stepanova). Participant in several national and international exhibitions. Held personal exhibition in Moscow in 1987.

Astvatsaturyan, Aknuny Arkadyevich, Leningrad (b. 1925). Merited Artist of RSFSR, winner of Repin State Prize of RSFSR. Graduated from Rostov Art School. In 1961 graduated from Mukhina Higher School of Industrial Design in Leningrad. Worked at Vosstaniye Factory, 1961–1965. Became artist in 1965 and Chief Artist of Leningrad Glassworks, 1975–1985. Has participated in several national and foreign exhibitions.

Bakhmetievs. Owners of glassworks at Nikol'skoye and Pestravka, in Penza region. (Portrait reproduced from the book *150 Years of the Factory of Prince Obolenski in Nikol'skoye,* St. Petersburg, 1914.)

1) **Alexei Ivanovich** (d. 1779). Reached rank of major in army. Received permission to build glassworks in 1763. Rebuilt under leadership of Yemelyan Pugachyov after 1773–1774 peasant war.

2) **Agafokleya Ivanovna.** Widow of Alexei Ivanovich. Owned glassworks from 1779 to 1802.

3) **Nikolai Alekseevich.** Lieutenant. Owned glassworks from 1802 to 1836.

4) **Alexei Nikolaievich** (1798–1861). *Hofmeister* (steward) of the Imperial court. Owned glassworks from 1836 to 1861.

5) **Anna Ivanovna.** Owned glassworks from 1861 to 1884. After her death, in accordance with her will, the glassworks passed to Alexander Dmitriyevich Obolensky, which he owned until 1917.

Barashevsky, Vasily (1755–1812). Engraver at St. Petersburg (later Imperial) Glassworks. Pupil (in 1770), apprentice (in 1792), and craftsman (in 1807).

Boem, Yelizaveta Merkuryevna (1843–1914). Artist. Studied at Society for the Encouragement of Artists. For her pencil drawings received silver medal award in 1865 and grand gold medal award in 1870 from Academy of Fine Arts. Her fourteen albums of silhouettes published in 1875 were reprinted in several American publications. Relative of manager of Dyat'kovo Crystal Works; helped design factory's products. Her works were praised for the "highly artistic reproduction of national style" at Chicago world's fair in 1893.

Bonafede, Yustinian (Justinian) Petrovich (1825–1866). Mosaicist and chemist. Of Italian descent. Came to Russia in 1851. Began working at the Imperial Glassworks in 1854. From 1857 to 1866 was Chief Chemist and also took charge of the newly-formed Mosaics Branch of the Academy of Fine Arts. The glass melting furnaces were completely overhauled under his direction.

Bonafede, Leopold (d. 1878). Worked with brother, Yustinian Bonafede. Chief Chemist of Imperial Glassworks from 1866 to 1878.

Brianchon. "Chemist specializing in making metal enamels;" a French subject. Head of enameling workshop laboratory at Imperial Glassworks from 1849 to 1854.

Byakov, Yuri Mikhailovich, Leningrad (b. 1938). Graduated in 1965 from Mukhina Higher School of Industrial Design in Leningrad. Employed since then as artist at Leningrad Glassworks. Participant in several national and international exhibitions.

Druzhinin, Pyotr. Student at School of Architecture from 1744 to 1752. In 1752 was sent to laboratory under direction of Mikhail Lomonosov to learn production of stained glass. Worked at St. Petersburg Glassworks, 1753–1773, as "master for making colored objects."

Fershtel, Christian. Engraver. In 1731 was invited to Yamburg glassworks rented by Elmsel. Dismissed in 1733. From 1736 to 1741 worked at St. Petersburg Glassworks.

Filatov, Vladimir Alexandrovich, Moscow (b. 1933). Merited Artist of RSFSR, winner of Repin State Prize of RSFSR. Graduated from Theatrical and Art School in Alma Ata in 1953. Graduated from Mukhina Higher School of Industrial Design in Leningrad in 1959; took a post-graduate course at Moscow Higher School of Industrial Design in 1965. Became artist in 1959 and has been Chief Artist of Gus Crystal Works since 1969. Became Chief Artist at Ministry for Production of Building Materials in 1969. Makes glass articles at Gus Crystal Works. Participant in several national and foreign exhibitions. Personal exhibition was held in Moscow in 1983.

Fomina, Lidiya Andreevna, Moscow (b. 1942). Works in co-authorship with T. P. Sazhin. Graduated from Higher School of Industrial Design in Moscow in 1967. Worked at Krasnyy Mai Glassworks, 1967–1969. Since 1970 has made glass articles (chandeliers, fountains, panels) for interior of various public buildings. Participant in several national and international exhibitions.

Frolov, Alexander. Cutter. Began working at Imperial Glassworks in 1792 and became master in 1830.

Fyodorov, Boris, Kalinin (b. 1948). Graduated from Mukhina Higher School of Industrial Design in Leningrad in 1976. Employed at Dyat'kovo Crystal Works. Since 1981 has been Chief Artist of Kalinin Glass Department. Participant in several national and foreign exhibitions. Awarded honorary certificate at fourth Quadriennale of Folk Arts of Socialist Countries in Erfurt.

Genkin, Joseph. Engraver. Born in Bohemia. In 1730 signed contract with Vasily Maltsov. Worked at glassworks in Mozhaysk district, 1730–1737; Gottlieb Stenzel's glassworks, 1737–1742; and Vasily Maltsov's glassworks, 1742–1748.

Goncharova, Natal'ya Mikhailovna, Leningrad (b. 1945). Graduated from Mukhina Higher School of Industrial Design in Leningrad in 1968. Since 1974 has been employed as artist at Leningrad Glassworks. Participant in several national and international exhibitions.

Gube, Johann (Ivan Frantsevich). Master of cutting and engraving; a Prussian subject. Worked at Imperial Glassworks under contract from 1836 to 1851. Received an award in 1848 for participating in interior decoration of Grand Kremlin Palace in Moscow.

Hartmann, Victor Alexandrovich (1834–1873). Architect. Graduated from Academy of Fine Arts in St. Petersburg in 1861. Worked in St. Petersburg from 1869 to 1871. Participated in decoration of All-Russian Industrial Exhibition in 1870 and first All-Russian Polytechnical Exhibition in Moscow in 1872.

Ibragimov, Fidail Mullaakhmetovich, Moscow (b. 1938). Graduated from Moscow Higher School of Industrial Design in 1966. Employed at Gus Crystal Works, 1966–1969. Since 1969 has been artist at Integrated Works of Applied Art of Moscow Organization of Artistic Foundation of RSFSR. Participant in several national and foreign exhibitions. Group exhibitions held in Moscow, Leningrad, and Lvov in 1980, 1984, and 1987.

Ivanov, Alexander Alekseevich, Leningrad (b. 1944). Graduated from Mukhina Higher School of Industrial Design in Leningrad in 1968. Worked at Krasnyy Gigant Glassworks in Penza region, 1968–1969. Taught at alma mater in 1968. Has participated in national and foreign exhibitions since 1966. Works as free-lance artist, making glass articles at Lvov Experimental Factory of Ceramics and Sculpture of Artistic Foundation of Ukrainian SSR. Specializes in creating decorative and monumental glass forms. Group exhibitions held in Lvov, Leningrad, and Moscow in 1980, 1984, and 1987.

Ivanov, Ivan Alekseevich (1779–1848). Artist. Began designing works of applied and decorative art in 1806. From 1815 to 1848 was Artistic Director of Imperial Glassworks. Designed many monumental works in first half of 19th century.

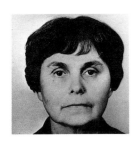

Jurgen, Leida Oskarovna, Leningrad (b. 1925). Merited Artist of RSFSR. Graduated from State Institute of Art of Estonian SSR in 1952. Began working at Leningrad Glassworks in 1955. Made numerous glass objects for mass production, as well as several unique decorative compositions. Participant in national and foreign exhibitions. Awarded gold medal at 1973 International Exhibition of China and Glass at Jablonec nad Nisou, Czechoslovakia. Solo exhibitions held in Tallinn and Leningrad in 1976.

Karamyshev, Ivan Feodorovich (d. 1873). Senior master of enameling workshop at Imperial Glassworks. Started working there in 1828, became a master in 1849, and worked as senior master from 1858 to 1873.

Karamyshev, Lev Maksimovich (1790–1836). Cutting and grinding master at Imperial Glassworks. Started work in 1802. Became a master in 1816. In 1830 was sent to Paris for training at French glassworks.

Left the job in 1833. Known as maker of sculptural glass items, vases and services.

Karamyshev, Yefrem Feodorovich (1752/56–1818). Began training in 1765 at St. Petersburg Glassworks. In 1775 worked as cutting and grinding master. Was sent to Britain in 1783, then returned, and from 1784 to 1788 studied chemistry and mineralogy in Britain. In 1789 became Chief Master of St. Petersburg Glassworks. In 1792 received award for the "decoration of rooms" with stained glass in Tsarskoye Selo. Received award in 1796 for decoration of Tavricheski Palace, and in 1800 for interior decoration of Mikhailovski Palace. In 1804 became inspector in charge of crafts at Imperial Glassworks.

Kartsev, Dmitry Alexandrovich. Chemist. Studied at Moscow University. Participated in Russian army's European campaigns, 1813–1814. Was employed at the Imperial Glassworks from 1832 to 1834.

Kasatkin, Vladimir Ivanovich, Gus' Khrustal'nyy (b. 1945). Engraver at Gus Crystal Works, 1964–1966. Graduated from Mukhina Higher School of Industrial Design in Leningrad in 1971. Artist at Gus Crystal Works since 1971. Participant in several national and foreign exhibitions.

Kitayev, Vasily Ivanovich (1778–1857). Began in 1790 as glass painter at Imperial Glassworks. In 1821 became a master at the painting shop.

Konerev, Ivan. Master in charge of "making compounds" at St. Petersburg Glassworks. In 1741 he said that, besides clear and green glass, he could make "red, black, white, cherry-colored, and cornflower blue" glass according to his own formulas. In 1751 was to have been sent to Mikhail Lomonosov for training, but for some unknown reason the scheme never materialized.

Korneyev, Vladimir Vasilevich, Gus' Khrustal'nyy (b. 1927). Merited Artist of RSFSR, winner of Repin State Prize of RSFSR. Graduated from Ryazan Art School, 1951, and from Mukhina Higher School of Industrial Design in Leningrad, 1960. Became artist in 1962, and has been Chief Artist at Gus Crystal Works since 1969. Participant in several national and foreign exhibitions. Awarded silver medal of International Exhibition of Glass and China in Jablonec nad Nisou, Czechoslovakia.

Kotov, Vladimir Ivanovich (b. 1944). Dyat'kovo, Bryansk region. Merited Artist of RSFSR, winner of Lenin YCL Prize. Graduated from Mukhina Higher School of Industrial Design in Leningrad in 1968. Employed since 1968 at Dyat'kovo Crystal Works (Chief Artist, 1975–1977). Made (together with I. Pyatkin) several decorative spatial light compositions of glass and crystal in architecture. Participant in several national and foreign exhibitions.

Koyets.
1) **Yulius.** Gunsmith. Of Swedish descent. Arrived in Russia in 1630 for military service. In 1634 received a license to build the first glassworks in Russia. He died the same year, however.

2) **Anton** (d. 1660). Yulius's son. Worked with "gunsmith" Ivan Falk to complete construction of glassworks in 1639. Pawned remaining part of glassworks to Falk in 1647.

3) **Peter.** Owned half of the glassworks in 1660. Sold his part to Andrei Minter in 1702.

Kozlova, Olga Ivanovna, Gus' Khrustal'nyy (b. 1942). Graduated from Zagorsk School of Industrial Design in 1960. Worked at Gus branch of State Institute of Glass, 1961–1965. Employed as artist at Gus Crystal Works since 1965. Participant in several national and foreign exhibitions.

Kurilov, Adolf Stepanovich, Gus' Khrustal'nyy (b. 1937). Graduated from Mukhina Higher School of Industrial Design in Moscow. Employed as artist at Gus Crystal Works since 1968. Participant in several Soviet and international exhibitions.

Lagutin, Stepan. Engraver. Born town of Ryl'sk. From 1732 to 1740 worked at Vasily Maltsov's glassworks near Moscow. Trained by Bohemian engraver, Joseph Genkin. In 1740 worked at Gottlieb Stenzel's glassworks near Moscow. Engraved glass purchased in Moscow, 1741–1742. In 1743 was employed at Nechayev's glassworks in Yaroslavl' and in 1748 began employment at Lonkarev's glassworks in the Mozhaysk District. From 1749 to 1756 worked at Maltsovs' glassworks near Moscow, from 1756 to 1765 at their glassworks in Gus' Khrustal'nyy in the Vladimir region, and from 1765 to 1775 at Bakhmetievs' glassworks in the Penza region.

Lerin, (?) Indrik. "Master of making figurines." A foreigner who came to Russia in 1670 with a team of so-called "Venetian" craftsmen. From 1670 to 1710 worked at Izmailovo glassworks near Moscow, where various vessels with "figurines" were made.

Levashov, Semyon Leontyevich (1761–1827). Master in charge of making compounds. Employed as workman (1771), apprentice (1784–1794), and master (1794–?) at St. Petersburg Glassworks. In 1807 became First Master of Imperial Glassworks. Visited Britain "to learn more about treatment of glass objects."

Lomonosov, Mikhail Vasilevich (1711–1765). Prominent Russian encyclopedic scientist, natural scientist, historian, poet, and artist; member of Academy of Sciences; founder of Moscow University. In 1753 he set up his own glassworks in Ust' Ruditsa near St. Petersburg, where tesserae for mosaics were made. Was in charge of the mosaics workshop of Academy of Sciences in St. Petersburg. Created a number of monumental mosaics, the best known being *The Battle of Poltava*. Developed formulas for various types of stained glass. Author of poetic work *On the Usefulness of Glass*. (Portrait: engraving by Johann Friedrich Moritz Schreyer, 18th century, courtesy State Historical Museum, Moscow.)

Machnev, Ivan Vasilevich, Dyat'kovo, Bryansk region (b. 1939). Graduated from Mukhina Higher School of Industrial Design in Leningrad, 1973. Employed as artist since 1975 at Dyat'kovo Crystal Works in Bryansk region. Participant in several national and foreign exhibitions. Solo exhibition held in Moscow in 1988.

Maltsovs. Owners of Russia's largest glassworks.
1) **Vasily.** Owned a glasshouse in the Mozhaysk District near Moscow from 1723 to 1746. Handed over management of glassworks to his sons, Akim and Alexander.

2) **Alexander Vasilevich** (d. 1751). With his brother took ownership of glassworks in the Mozhaysk District in 1746. Following the division of property in 1750, moved his part of glassworks to town of Radutino in Trubchevsk District near Bryansk.

3) **Yevdokiya.** Alexander's widow. Owned Radutino glassworks beginning in 1751. Later moved it to village of Raditsa in same district.

4) **Akim Vasilevich** (d. 1788). Owned glassworks in Mozhaysk District in 1746 with his brother. Moved his part of glassworks in 1756 to Vladimir region to found the crystal works in Gus' Khrustal'nyy as well as a number of small glassworks in neighborhood. Raised to rank of nobility in 1775.

5) **Marya Vasilyevna**, Akim's widow, owned glassworks of both branches of Maltsov family in Vladimir and Bryansk Districts in 1788. Actively built new works, including Dyat'kovo Crystal Works, the largest in Russia, in 1793.

6) **Ivan Akimovich,** son of Akim and Marya (1768–1853). In 1804 inherited 10 glassworks and built several new ones. Was active in building first sugar refineries in Russia. Took part in several All-Russia industrial exhibitions. (Portrait: oil on canvas, unknown artist with initials "A. T.," 1820s, courtesy State Historical Museum, Moscow.)

7) **Sergei Ivanovich** (1809–1893), son of Ivan Akimovich, Major General, inherited glassworks in the Bryansk District. Built crystal palace in the Crimea (Simeiz), several steel works, the first steam engine and railway car works in Russia and also numerous steamships and barges. Contemporaries described his industrial area as "America in Russia." In 1875 he went bankrupt and organized the trade and manufacturing company of Maltsov glassworks. Ended his business activity in 1884. (Photograph, courtesy State Historical Museum, Moscow.)

8) **Sergei Akimovich,** son of Akim, purchased glassworks in the Vladimir region in 1817, including the Gus Crystal Works, from his brother Ivan Akimovich.

9) **Ivan Sergeyevich** (1807–1880). Privy councillor, owner of glassworks in Vladimir region. Secretary of Russian Embassy in Teheran. Escaped to safety during massacre of Russian Embassy staff in 1829. On return, was actively involved in the affairs of Gus glassworks. Being childless, left his glassworks to his nephew, Yuri Stepanovich Nechayev.

10) **Yuri Stepanovich Nechayev-Maltsov** (1834–1913). In 1880 became last owner of Maltsov glassworks. Also owner of gold mines, collector, and patron of art. Financed construction of Museum of Fine Arts in Moscow and donated to that institution a collection of Egyptian antiquities. Built St. George's Cathedral in Gus' Khrustal'nyy, engaging services of best architects and painters for its interior decoration. The cathedral now houses a museum of glass. (Portrait: oil on canvas, N. Kramskoi, courtesy State Pushkin Museum of Fine Arts, Moscow.)

Manelis, Yuri Mikhailovich, Leningrad (b. 1945). Graduated from Mukhina Higher School of Industrial Design in Leningrad in 1975. Became employed at Vosstaniye Works in 1975; was made Chief Artist there in 1976. Participant in several national and foreign exhibitions. Solo exhibition held in Leningrad in 1987. Group exhibition of his works arranged in 1988.

Marshumova, Irina Mikhailovna, Kalinin (b. 1937). Graduated in 1964 from Mukhina Higher School of Industrial Design in Leningrad. Employed at Kalinin Works since 1967; became Chief Artist there in 1975. Participant in several national and international exhibitions. Lampwork artist.

Mennart, Johann. Engraver. Worked at A. D. Menshikov's glassworks in Yamburg near St. Petersburg from 1718 to 1728.

Menshikov, Alexander Danilovich (1673–1729). Prince, general, associate and friend of Emperor Peter the Great. From 1710 to 1727 owned Yamburg and Zhabino glassworks near St. Petersburg. (Portrait: engraving by Simon Londiony, courtesy State Historical Museum, Moscow.)

Mikhailov, Pavel Ivanovich (b. 1830). Graduated from Institute of Technology in 1844. Pupil of mosaicist Rafaelli in the Mosaics Workshop. Employed in chemical department of Imperial Glassworks from 1857. Took part in several world's fairs. Dismissed for health reasons in 1869.

Morso. Chemist, master of glass compounding in "dish tent" of Imperial Glassworks. Began employment there in 1847. Became master in 1852.

Moryakin, Ilya Yegorovich. Master. Began employment in cutting and grinding workshop of Imperial Glassworks in 1804. Worked as master from 1831 to 1844.

Mukhina, Vera Ignatyevna (b. Riga 1889, d. 1953). People's Artist of USSR, full member of Academy of Fine Arts of USSR. Studied in K. Yuon's and I. Mashkov's studios in Moscow, 1909–1913, and in Bourdelle's studio in Paris. Started working with glass in 1938. Made several crystal articles at Krasnyy Gigant Works, 1938–1939. Became Artistic Director of Experimental Shop at Leningrad Mirror Factory (later Leningrad Glassworks) in 1940. Main works are vases *Turnip, Lotus, Aster,* and *Campanula* (1940–1941) and sculptures *Torso* and *Grief* (1940).

Muratov, Vladimir Sergeyevich, Gus' Khrustal'nyy (b. 1929). Merited Artist of RSFSR, winner of Repin State Prize of RSFSR, Corresponding Member of Academy of Fine Arts of USSR. Graduated from Odessa Art School, 1957, and from Mukhina Higher School of Industrial Design in Leningrad, 1965. Employed at Gus Crystal Works since 1966. Participant in several national and foreign exhibitions since 1964.

Awarded 1972 Gold Medal of Academy of Fine Arts of USSR, and won second prize at Quadriennale of Folk Arts of Socialist Countries in Erfurt in 1977.

Muravlyov, Pyotr Alekseevich. Master of compounding crystal and stained glass at Dyat'kovo Crystal Works. Received citation in 1848 for his part in the All-Russia Industrial Exhibition.

Murinov, Ivan Ivanovich. Glass painter. Started work at Imperial Glassworks in 1855; in 1872 became master in "painting workshop." From 1894 to 1901 was in charge of artistic department of Imperial China and Glass Works.

Neupokoyev, Pyotr Savich (1791–1855). Graduated from Mining Military School. Joined Imperial Glassworks, 1809. Was Chief Master there, 1830–1849.

Nikitin, Alexander. Cutter. "Cutting and grinding master" of Imperial Glassworks. Began employment there in 1827; became master in 1851. Awarded silver medal for participation in Paris fair.

Orlovs. Owners of glassworks.
1) **Fyodor Grigoryevich.** Count. One of five Orlov brothers who took part in 1762 palace coup which brought Catherine II to Russian throne. Mentioned in 1797 as owner of glassworks in Kaluga province.

2) **Mikhail Feodorovich** (1788–1842). Major General. Took part in 1812 Patriotic War and Russian army's European campaigns, 1813–1814. Accepted surrender of Paris. Participated in Decembrists' liberation movement. In 1814 became owner of glassworks in village of Milyutino of Kaluga province. Married Ye N. Rayevskaya, granddaughter of Mikhail Lomonosov. After suppression of Decembrists' uprising in 1825 was exiled to village of Milyutino and was actively involved in affairs of glassworks. Set up glass enameling workshop in Moscow. Actively participated in national industrial fairs. After his death, glassworks became property of A. D. Zalivskaya, and after 1849, it ceased to exist. (Portrait: oil on canvas, E. Pljushar, 1830, courtesy State Historical Museum, Moscow.)

3) **Yakov Petrovich.** Master of Dyat'kovo Crystal Works. Received award in 1849 for participation in All-Russia industrial fair "for invention of various forms and colors of crystal objects."

Ostroumov, Adolf Mikhailovich, Leningrad (b. 1934). Merited Artist of RSFSR, winner of Repin State Prize of RSFSR. Graduated from Mukhina Higher School of Industrial Design in Leningrad in 1960. Studied in Czechoslovakia, 1959–1960. Employed as artist at Leningrad Glassworks since 1960. Participant in several national and international exhibitions.

Pavlov, Alexander. Master of Imperial Glassworks. In 1835 became master of "Mosaics Department" at Academy of Fine Arts. Was master at the "dish tent" of Imperial Glassworks, 1861–1890. Took part in making glass objects displayed at World's Fair in Paris.

Petukhov, Sergei Petrovich. Industrial engineer. Chief Chemist of Imperial Glassworks. Graduated from Institute of Technology in St. Petersburg. Began work at Imperial Glassworks under contract in 1869. Was Chief Chemist, 1878–1892. Particularly successful in producing glass for stained glass; invented several glass compounds. Authored monograph, *Glassmaking*, in 1898.

Pilz, Joseph (b. 1720). Engraver. From 1766, cutting master at St. Petersburg Glassworks.

Pivovarov, Vasily. Engraving master. Apprentice at Yamburg glassworks in 1728. Last mentioned in 1770 when in charge of cutting workshop at St. Petersburg Glassworks.

Pogrebnoy, Vladimir Konstantinovich, Dyat'kovo, Bryansk region (b. 1948). Graduated from Mukhina Higher School of Industrial Design in Leningrad, 1976. Employed at Dyat'kovo Crystal Works. Participant in several national and foreign exhibitions.

Põld, Helle Martinovna (1928–1984). Graduated from State Institute of Art of Estonian SSR. Taught at Mukhina Higher School of Industrial Design in Leningrad, 1953–1956. Artist at Leningrad Glassworks from 1956. Participant in several national and foreign exhibitions.

Potemkin, Grigori Aleksandrovich (1739–1791). Owner of glassworks, Russian statesman and military leader, General Field Marshal (from 1784). Took part in 1762 palace coup and became a favorite of Catherine II. In 1777 received state glassworks in village of Naziya "for perpetual and hereditary ownership." In 1783 moved glassworks to village of Ozerki. After his death glassworks again became state owned and was named an Imperial Glassworks. (Portrait: engraving after Lampi, 1789, courtesy State Historical Museum, Moscow.)

Ratmanov, Stepan Ivanovich (1799–1859). Cutter at Imperial Glassworks. Began working there in 1804, became cutter in cutting and grinding shop in 1820, and became master, 14th class, in 1837.

Rogov, Yevgheny Ivanovich, Gus' Khrustal'nyy (b. 1918). People's Artist of RSFSR, winner of Repin State Prize of RSFSR. Employed at Gus Crystal Works since 1936, specializing in deep etching. Became artist at the works in 1950. In his objects, developed a line of plant ornamentation in cut crystal and glass which is traditional at the Gus Works. Participated in several national and foreign exhibitions.

Rossi, Karl Ivanovich (1775–1849). Russian architect. Authored many architectural ensembles in St. Petersburg, including Mikhailovski Palace (now Russian Museum), Alexandrinski Theatre, ensembles of Palace Square, Square of the Arts, Architect Rossi Street. Artistic Director (Inventor), Imperial Glassworks, 1813–1819.

Ryazanova, Svetlana Grigoryevna (b. 1927). Merited Artist of RSFSR. Studied at Moscow Higher School of Industrial Design, 1945–1948. Entered Moscow Institute of Applied and Decorative Art, 1949. Graduated from Mukhina Higher School of Industrial Design in Leningrad, 1955. Worked with Integrated Works of Applied Art in Moscow, 1960–1969. Made models for the Krasnyy Mai, Sverdlov Glassworks, and Dyat'kovo Crystal Works, to mention a few. Started making glass articles in 1970 for interior decoration of public buildings (in co-authorship with G. Antonova and A. Stepanova). Participant in several national and foreign exhibitions. Her exhibition (together with G. Antonova) was held in Moscow in 1987.

Savelyeva, Lyubov Ivanovna, Moscow (b. 1940). Free-lance artist who has worked with glass since 1966. Graduated from the Moscow Higher Art Industrial Secondary School, 1966. Member of the Artist's Union of the USSR since 1970. Participated in several international exhibitions, including the 1979 Corning exhibition, "New Glass," and "Glass, Image, Transparency" in Moscow and Kiev. Received awards from the Moscow Region and Moscow City Artist's Union in 1980 and 1981.

Sazhin, Timur Petrovich, Moscow (b. 1943). Works in co-authorship with L. A. Fomina. Graduated from Higher School of Industrial Design in Moscow in 1967. Worked at Krasnyy Mai Glassworks, 1967–1969. Since 1970 has made glass articles (chandeliers, fountains, panels) for interior of various public buildings. Participant in several national and international exhibitions.

Schot, Johann. Maker of compounds, Saxon. Worked at Elmsel's Lavinsky glassworks until 1738; later transferred to St. Petersburg Glassworks. Worked at Gottlieb Stenzel's (formerly Koyet's) glassworks, 1741–1742. In 1743 worked at Vasily Maltsov's glassworks in Mozhaysk District.

Semyonov, Dmitry Kuzmich (1796–1863). Began work in "dish tent" of Imperial Glassworks in 1809; became blowing master in 1825. Sent to Paris in 1830 to study operation of French glassworks. Last mentioned in 1845.

Serebryannikov, Pavel Grigoryevich. Industrial engineer. Graduated from Institute of Technology in St. Petersburg. Began employment at Imperial Glassworks as industrial engineer in 1853.

Shevchenko, Victor Yakovlevich (b. 1935). Merited Artist of RSFSR, Moscow. Graduated from Mukhina Higher School of Industrial Design in 1961; took a postgraduate course there in 1966. Worked at Dyat'kovo Crystal Works, 1961–1975. In 1975 became employed at Krasnyy Mai Works, Kalinin region, where he was Chief Artist, 1975–1982. Awarded certificate of the Quadriennale of Folk Arts of Socialist Countries in Erfurt in 1974.

Shushkanov, Dmitry Nikolayevich, Moscow (b. 1923). Merited Artist of RSFSR, full member of Academy of Fine Arts of USSR. Works with L. N. Shushkanova. Graduated from Moscow Institute of Applied and Decorative Art. Started working with glass in 1965. Decorated with silver medal of Academy of Fine Arts of USSR. Received second prize at first Quadriennale of Folk Arts of Socialist Countries in Erfurt in 1974. Solo exhibitions held in Moscow in 1978 and 1984.

Shushkanova, Lyudmila Nikolayevna, Moscow (b. 1926). People's Artist of RSFSR. Graduated from Moscow Institute of Applied and Decorative Art in 1951. Works in co-authorship with D. N. Shushkanov. Participant in numerous national and international exhibitions. Winner of international awards at International Exhibition of Ceramics in Geneva (1965) and Quadriennale of Folk Arts of Socialist Countries in Erfurt in 1974. Solo exhibitions were held in Moscow in 1978 and 1984.

Smirnov, Boris Alexandrovich, Leningrad (1903–1987). Merited Artist of RSFSR, winner of Repin State Prize, Professor. Graduated from Leningrad Academy of Fine Arts in 1927. Worked at Leningrad Glassworks, 1948–1967. Head of Chair of Ceramics and Glass at Mukhina Higher School of Industrial Design in Leningrad, 1952–1963. Also taught at Moscow Higher School of Industrial Design. As one of the founders of Soviet glassmaking, he trained an entire generation of glass artists. Participated in several national and foreign exhibitions. Solo exhibitions held in Moscow and Leningrad, 1976. Wrote several books and articles on problems of creative endeavor.

Sobolev, Nikolai. Cutter. Started working at Imperial Glassworks in 1827. Became senior cutting master in 1856. Received award in 1866 for preparing a collection for Moscow Industrial Fair.

Tikhomirova, Natal'ya Borisovna, Leningrad (b. 1946). Winner of Repin State Prize of RSFSR. Graduated from Mukhina Higher School of Industrial Design in Leningrad in 1970. Employed as artist at Leningrad Glassworks since 1970. Participant in several national and international exhibitions.

Thomas de Thomon, Jean (1760–1813). Frenchman. Began working in Russia in 1799. Designed numerous architectural ensembles in St. Petersburg. Artistic Director (Inventor), Imperial Glassworks, 1804–1813.

Travkin, Ivan Nikolayevich (1860–1904). Engraver at Maltsovs' crystal works in Gus' Khrustal'nyy. Said to have made best engraved objects of the works in late 19th century.

Tsvetnikov, Dmitry. Grinding master. Worked at Menshikov's glassworks in Yamburg in 1716. Worked in Moscow in 1745 grinding glass objects from Gottlieb Stenzel's glassworks.

Ullmann, Matthias. Engraver. Born in Czech town of Lipa. Arrived in Russia through the port of Archangel in 1688. Later worked in Moscow engraving imported glass. From 1690 to 1710 was engraver at Izmailovo glassworks. Left the job when glassworks ceased to make glass objects of artistic value.

Uryadova Natal'ya Vitaliyevna, Moscow (b. 1948). Graduated from Mukhina Higher School of Industrial Design in Leningrad in 1972. Employed as artist at Ivanitsevsky Glassworks, 1972–1977, and at Lytkarinsky Optic Glassworks, 1977–1985. Employed at Moscow Crystal Works since 1985.

Uspensky, Alexei Alexandrovich (1892–1941). Graduated in 1917 from Central School of Technical Drawing (formerly Stieglitz School). Worked at Experimental Shop of Leningrad Mirror Factory (Leningrad Glassworks), 1940–1941.

Vershinin, Alexander Petrovich (d. 1822). Chief Master of Nikol'skoye-Pestravka Glassworks owned by Bakhmetievs from 1795 to 1822. Awarded gold watch by Emperor Alexander I in St. Petersburg in 1807. His signed works include double-walled glasses and glasses decorated with portraits of heroes of 1812 Patriotic War. He also designed crystal services.

Veselkin, Nikolai. Apprentice of "cutting and grinding workshop" of Imperial Glassworks. Participated in making glass objects for 1856 Industrial Exhibition in Moscow.

Voilokov, Dementy. Engraver. In 1728 worked at Menshikov's glassworks in Yamburg and later, till 1738, at St. Petersburg Glassworks.

Voronikhin, Andrei Nikiforovich (1759–1814). Russian architect coming from a family of serfs owned by Baron Stroganov. Worked in St. Petersburg, Pavlovsk, and Peterhof (Kazan Cathedral in St. Petersburg 1801–1811, the Mining Institute 1806–1811). Designed various items from Imperial Glassworks.

Voronkov, Vasily Andreyevich (b. 1799). Commissar at workshop for "cutting, grinding, and treating mirror glass." Began working at Imperial Glassworks in 1808; appointed Commissar there in 1825. Last mentioned in 1840.

Yanovskaya, Yekaterina Vasilyevna, Leningrad (b. 1913). Merited Artist of RSFSR. Graduated from Moscow Institute of Applied and Decorative Art in 1949. Has worked at Leningrad Glassworks since 1959 (Chief Artist until 1975). Awarded 1983 silver medal of Academy of Fine Arts of USSR, and Grand Prix of the 1976 International Exhibition of Glass and China at Jablonec nad Nisou, Czechoslovakia. Solo exhibitions held in Leningrad, 1979, and in Moscow, 1980.

Zaitsev, Vyacheslav Sergeyevich, Gus' Khrustal'nyy (b. 1954). Graduated in 1982 from Mukhina Higher School of Industrial Design in Leningrad. Employed at Gus Crystal Works since 1982.

Zhirnov, Vasily Timofeyevich. Blower, master of "dish tent" of Imperial Glassworks, 1811–1860.

Zhokhov, Vladimir Petrovich. Beryozovka, Grodno region (b. 1933). Graduated from Mukhina Higher School of Industrial Design in Leningrad in 1960. Employed at Krasnyy Mai Glassworks in Kalinin region, 1960–1963. Has worked at Neman glassworks in Belorussian SSR since 1967. Participant in several national and foreign exhibitions. Awarded the Gold Medal at the International Exhibition of Glass and China in Jablonec nad Nisou in Czechoslovakia.

Zubanov, Maxim. Cutting and engraving master at Maltsovs' crystal works in Gus' Khrustal'nyy. Received award in 1856 for dish presented to Emperor Alexander II from Vladimir region during his coronation. His name is associated at the glassworks with the best cutting works of the late 19th and early 20th centuries.

Zubov, Mikhail. Blower, master of "dish tent" of Imperial Glassworks in the second half of 19th century. He distinguished himself by his large-size glass objects.

Bibliography

Note: Although the titles are cited in English, most of these sources appear in the Russian language. The bibliography is printed as received from the authors.

Asharina (1972)
N. A. Asharina, "Goblet with Emblems," *Nauka i Zhizn*, 1972, pp. 48–49.

Asharina (1973)
N. Asharina, "Humor of the Village of Izmailovo," *Nauka i Zhizn*, 1973, no. 11, pp. 151–153.

Asharina (1974a)
N. A. Asharina, "Russian Folk Glass of the 18th Century," *Dekorativnoye Iskusstvo SSSR*, 1974, no. 1, pp. 56–58.

Asharina (1974b)
N. A. Asharina, "Yamburg Glass," *Dekorativnoye Iskusstvo SSSR*, 1974, no. 5, pp. 52–53.

Asharina (1974c)
N. Asharina, "Foreign Glassmakers in Russia in the 17th–18th Centuries," *Ars Vitraria* (Jablonec nad Nisou), no. 5, 1974, pp. 24–33. In Czech.

Asharina (1978a)
N. A. Asharina, "Glass," in T. I. Dul'kina, *Russian Ceramics and Glass of the 18th–19th Centuries. Collection of the State History Museum*, Moscow, 1978, pp. 11–103m and 285–296.

Asharina (1978b)
N. A. Asharina, "Russian Artistic Glass" *Transactions of the State History Museum*, Moscow, no. 47, 1978, pp. 66–88.

Asharina (1980)
N. Asharina, "Russian Engraved Glass of the Eighteenth Century," *Journal of Glass Studies*, v. 22, 1980, pp. 53–77. In English.

Asharina (1981)
N. Asharina, *Russian Artistic Glass of the 17th–20th Centuries*, Moscow?, 1981.

Asharina (1986)
N. A. Asharina, "Russian Glassworks of the 17th–18th Centuries," *Transactions of the State History Museum*, no. 62, Moscow, 1986, pp. 3–15 and 45–61.

Asharina (1987)
N. Asharina, *Russian Decorative Art: 12th to Early 20th Century in the Historical Museum, Moscow*, Leningrad, 1987. In English.

Asharina (1988)
N. A. Asharina, "The Trends in Development of Art Nouveau in Maltsov's Glass at the Turn of the 20th Century," *Artist, Object, Fashion (Art Gallery)*, Moscow, 1988, pp. 262–272.

Baklanova (1928)
N. A. Baklanova, "Glassworks in the 17th-Century Moscow State," *Transactions of the State History Museum*, no. 4, Moscow, 1928, pp. 119–141.

Batanova and Voronov (1964)
G. Batanova and N. Voronov, *Soviet Decorative Glass*, Leningrad, 1964.

Catalog: Antonova (1987)
Galina Antonova, Moscow, 1987.

Catalog: Farbglass (1989)
Farbglass, Porzelan und Keramik aus Russland, Bonn, 1989.

Catalog: Glass, Image, Space (1987)
Nikolaeva, *Glass, Image, Space*, Moscow, 1987.

Catalog of State Hermitage (1967)
Artistic Glass, Leningrad, 1967.

Catalog of State Hermitage (1979)
Monuments of Russian Artistic Culture of the 10th–Early 20th Centuries in the Collection of the State Hermitage, Moscow, 1979.

Catalog of State Hermitage (1983–1984)
Dos siglos de arto Ruso 18–19. Pinture y artes aplicadas, Caracas, Mexico, and Havana, 1983–1984.

Catalog of State Hermitage (1984)
Russian Art of the Baroque Epoch, Leningrad, 1984.

Catalog of State Hermitage (1987)
Russia and France: The Age of Enlightenment, Leningrad, 1987.

Catalog of State Hermitage (1989)
Russian and Soviet Art Glass, Leningrad, 1989.

Catalog: Riihimäki (1984)
L. Kazakova, *Soviet Glass: Substance and Form*, Riihimäki, 1984.

Catalog: Ryazanova (1987)
Svetlana Ryazanova: Glass, Moscow, 1987.

Catalog: Yanovskaya (1980)
M. M. Dubova, *Ekaterina Vasil'evna Ianovskia: Glass*, Moscow, 1980.

Kachalov (1959)
N. Kachalov, *Glass*, Moscow, 1959.

Kantor (1981)
K. Kantor, *Ludmila and Dmitry Shushkanov*, Moscow, 1981.

Kazakova (1973)
L. V. Kazakova, *Gus' Khrystal'nyy*, Moscow, 1973.

Kazakova (1980)
L. V. Kazakova, *Vladimir Muratov: Master of Soviet Art*, Moscow, 1980.

Kazakova (1984)
L. V. Kazakova, "Glass," in *Soviet Decorative Art, 1917–1945*, Moscow, 1984, pp. 120–132.

Liven (1901)
G. Liven, *A Guide to the Study of Peter the Great and the Gallery of Jewelry*, St. Petersburg, 1901.

Makarenko (1917)
N. E. Makarenko, *Lomonosov's Mosaic Works*, Petrograd, 1917.

Makarov (1949)
V. K. Makarov, *Lomonosov's Mosaics*, Leningrad, 1949.

Makarov (1950)
V. K. Makarov, *Lomonosov's Artistic Heritage: Mosaics*, Moscow and Leningrad, 1950.

Malinina (1983)
T. A. Malinina, "Materials on the History of the Petersburg Glassworks," *Transactions of the State Hermitage*, no. 23, Leningrad, 1983, pp. 165–170.

Malinina (1985)
T. A. Malinina, "On Some of the Imperial Glassworks Services of the 19th Century," in *Russian Culture and Art in the 19th Century*, Leningrad, 1985, pp. 101–113.

Malinina and Sapunov (1989)
T. A. Malinina and B. V. Sapunov, "The Influence of Ancient Russian Art on the Products of the Imperial Glassworks in the Second Half of the 19th Century," *The Collection at the Origins of Russian Culture (the 12th–17th Centuries)*, Leningrad, 1989.

Nikolaeva (1978)
N. Nikolaeva, *Mirona Grabar*, Moscow, 1978.

Pavlinskaya (1980)
A. Pavlinskaya, *Boris Alexandrovich Smirnov*, Leningrad, 1980.

Price List (1903)
"Price List of the Dyat'kovo Crystal Works of the Maltsov Works Joint-Stock Company," 1903.

Prokof'ev (1970)
E. Prokof'ev, *Russian Cut Glass: The Goose-Khrystalny Cut-Glassworks*, Leningrad, 1970.

Rachuk (1975)
E. G. Rachuk, *Soviet Sulphide — Zinc Glass*, Moscow, 1975.

Rachuk (1980)
E. G. Rachuk, *Dyat'kovo Crystal*, Moscow, 1980.

Rachuk (1982)
E. Rachuk, *Soviet Colored Glass*, Moscow, 1982.

Shchapova (1972)
Yu. L. Shchapova, *Glass of Kiev Rus*, Moscow, 1972.

Shelkovnikov (1960)
B. A. Shelkovnikov, "Russian Glass of the Eighteenth Century," *Journal of Glass Studies*, v. 2, 1960, pp. 95–111. In English.

Shelkovnikov (1962)
B. A. Shelkovnikov, *Artistic Glass*, Leningrad, 1962.

Shelkovnikov (1964)
B. A. Shelkovnikov, "Russian Glass in the First Half of the Nineteenth Century," *Journal of Glass Studies*, v. 6, 1964, pp. 101–122. In English.

Shelkovnikov (1967)
B. A. Shelkovnikov, "Russian Glass in the Second Half of the Nineteenth Century," *Journal of Glass Studies*, v. 9, 1967, pp. 122–128. In English.

Shelkovnikov (1969)
B. A. Shelkovnikov, *Russian Artistic Glass*, Leningrad, 1969.

Stepanyan (1978)
N. Stepanyan, *Victor Shevchenko: The Free Plastics of Glass*, Moscow, 1978.

Tatevosova (1987)
A. A. Tatevosova, "Masters of the Petersburg Glassworks in the Second Half of the 18th Century and the First Half of the 19th Century," *Commerce, Industry, and Town in Russian, 17th–19th Centuries*, Moscow, 1987, p. 176.

Voronov (1981)
N. V. Voronov, *Soviet Glass*, Leningrad, 1981.

Voronov and Dubova (1974)
N. V. Voronov and M. M. Dubova, *Diamond Facets*, Leningrad, 1974.

Voronov and Dubova (1984)
N. V. Voronov and M. M. Dubova, *Neva Crystal*, Leningrad, 1984.

Voronov and Rachuk (1973)
N. V. Voronov and E. G. Rachuk, *Soviet Glass*, Leningrad, 1973.

Yaglova (1959)
N. T. Yaglova, "Artistic Glass of Nemtshinov's Glassworks in the 18th Century," *Transactions of the State Russian Museum*, no. 4, Leningrad, 1959.